LET JUSTICE ROLL DOWN

John Perkins

BakerBooks

a division of Baker Publishing Group
Grand Rapids, Michigan

Published by Baker Books
a division of Baker Publishing Group
P.O. Box 6287, Grand Rapids, MI 49516-6287
www.bakerbooks.com

Baker Books edition published 2014
ISBN 978-0-8010-1815-2

Previously published by Regal Books

Printed in the United States of America

Library of Congress Cataloging Card No. 74-30172

16   17   18   19   20   21   22   9   8   7   6   5   4   3

Dedicated to Vera Mae, my wife, and to Spencer (deceased), Joanie, Phillip, Derek, Deborah, Wayne, Priscilla and Betty, my children.

Let justice roll down like waters,
And righteousness like an ever-flowing stream.

Amos 5:24, *RSV*

Contents

Past the Noise

Well, Regal Books said that it was between President Jimmy Carter and I as to who would write the foreword to *Let Justice Roll Down*. You'll have to settle for me. I'm not sure what Jimmy had going on, but I would drop virtually anything in the world—short of my own funeral—for John Perkins. Of course, I've never been president yet, either.

It's sort of like writing a foreword for your father, even though John and I don't share much in common by way of DNA, skin tone or hair style. But I'm not alone as his "son." John Perkins is a spiritual father to thousands of people, from punk kids and culture-savvy pastors to urban gangsters and activist theologians. Just as Mother Teresa raised up a family of orphans and outcasts, Papa John has fathered a ragtag and dysfunctional spiritual family as diverse as the kingdom of God. As one who was raised without a father, I recognize the gift of John as a father in this dad-hungry world—a father who is paternal without being patronizing. He loves and believes in this generation and in becoming the Church we dream of that will bring the change we want in the world.

For others of us, John Perkins has been a prophetic figure, a voice in the wilderness, like Moses leading an exodus people to a promised land. For many of his peers, John has carried on the torch of the civil rights movement with great integrity, careful to never sever the personal conversion from the social conversion.

He has led many over-churched souls to the streets where the gospel has come to life. And he has led many tired and thirsty fellow strugglers to an oasis of community where they have found living water. He has led folks who have written volumes of books and folks who have never read a word at all to the Word of life that transcends the pages of academia. And he has led us all with such humility that as we arrive at the secret promises of community, reconciliation and justice, we are able to say, "we did it ourselves."

Now, don't be fooled. John Perkins is also "Dr. Perkins," a legend so well respected that there are buildings and streets named after him. Although he dropped out of school, Dr. Perkins has more honorary degrees than I have T-shirts (in fact, I've been meaning to get on him about that to see if he might practice a little "redistribution" with those degrees). Yet while he's got the "Dr." thing down, he has the cleverness to know that God chooses the foolish things to confound the wise and the weak things to shame the strong. That's the Dr. Perkins that can float seamlessly between the addicts and politicians, the palaces and ghettoes, the halls of academia and the streets of injustice.

I'm amazed at what John gets away with. I guess that's one of the fruits that come with age: You can say what you want and not have to waste time sugarcoating the truth. You can hear in his voice the sassiness of the prophets but also the gentleness of a grandfather. This is part of his charm and the covert innocence that has allowed him to affect and infect so much of our society without getting killed (so far). Many times, with a glisten in his eyes and a smirk on his face, I've heard him say things such as, "We've got the best politicians . . . that money can buy." And I remember that same prophetic smile on his face as we went to jail together—not in the civil rights protests decades past, but only a year ago when we were singing those old spirituals and praying the Lord's prayer outside the Capitol to decry a national budget that turned the Beatitudes upside down as it blessed the rich and sent the poor away empty.

John cries out with the prophets, "Let justice roll down," and yet he will surprise you with his grace. I remember hearing one fellow share how he told John about his racist mother and, after listening intently, John said, "Does your mother like blueberries? Let's go visit her." And they did, fully armed with a bowl of berries. It is that sort of childlike love that our world is starving for. There is no doubt that we need justice to roll down like water; those words of the prophets drip from Perkins's tongue. And yet justice without grace still leaves us thirsty. Justice without reconciliation falls short of the gospel of Jesus. Love fills in the gaps of justice. John has lived for us what it looks like when justice and reconciliation kiss. After all, he did not just call for an end to the hate crimes of the Klu Klux Klan, but he became friends with a reborn Klansman.

Not long ago, I remember hearing that John had been invited to speak at one of the edgy, mostly white and academic conferences that used a lot of fancy multimedia and spectacular technology. He just got up and told his story. All the lights and hoorah were struck dumb. Past the noise of Christendom, the whisper of the Spirit could be heard. When you finish this book, you'll feel that dazzling tranquility—like after riding a good roller coaster when you just sit still, trying to take it all in. John Perkins has seen the loops, the dips, the bumps and thrills of life that bring tears to your eyes and butterflies to your stomach. He has held on for the ride. He has lived the Jesus adventure to its fullest in the front seat with his eyes wide open and his hands in the air.

I've heard it said, "If you want to know what someone believes, watch how they live." Each of us is a living epistle. Our lives shout what we believe, sometimes even louder than our words. So often, people cannot even hear our words past the noise of our lives.

In these pages is the story of a life well lived, a life that has become a proclamation of the Good News. Listen to John's life and allow it to draw you closer to Jesus, and closer to the poor . . . the Gospel according to John Perkins.

Shane Claiborne
Founding Member, The Simple Way
Author, *The Irresistible Revolution*
Board Member, The Christian Community
Development Association

Preface

Every Christian individual and every Christian group has a testimony. But the reason I feel that our testimony ought to go forward and be read by the Church is based upon a scene in our society today that is both frightening and beautiful.

I see today a beautiful evangelical Christian religious awakening in America. Recent political events have caused Americans to face crisis, to look within ourselves. And the deep sense of the problems have caused many to look out for a basic faith, something that will make things right, something that will anchor us back in the sheltered harbor of the justice and morality and goodness for which we long.

But I think many of us want forgiveness without repentance. I sense this so much as I try to establish relationships with my white brethren in the South. I find that they want my relationship, but they want more to quickly forget the brutality and the injustice that their people put upon many of us in the name of Christianity. And that's the frightening part.

Ours is not a story of bitterness—it is a story of love and the triumphs of the God of love. But it is a story carved out of the realities of violence and poverty, ending not in some sugarcoated sense of brotherly love but the deep conviction that only the power of Christ's crucifixion on the cross and the glory of His resurrection can heal the deep racial wounds in both black and white people in America.

Unless we see the depth of our need and unless we see the cross as the only answer, then we could see this wave of evangelical awakening someday turn into a wave of repression. For what is happening in the religious disputes of today and what happened in Nazi Germany prove that there is nothing more dangerous than latent religious prejudice and racism festering for a time beneath the surface of a light religious zeal only to explode later in violence, death and hatred.

For someone to think that he can forget the brutality and injustice of a system because of some light revival and worship is self-deception. It will take more than that.

I know, because for repentance and forgiveness to work in my life, God had to see me through months of agony and pain after being beaten almost to death. The Lord had to lead me through a great time of soul-searching. And it wasn't until I could look at a Mississippi Highway Patrolman, fully uniformed and ready for service, and look at him without feeling a sense of bitterness, that I could really begin to relate my faith in a creative way to the task of reconciliation and evangelism.

I have overcome that sense of bitterness in my own heart—even though it was caused by my enemy. God had to replace it with His love.

So I find it hard to believe in forgiveness without deep repentance. Yet, I believe that we are facing the same type of situation King Josiah faced with the nation of Israel. The rise of an evangelical faith corresponds to the rediscovering of the book of the law. We are rediscovering the truth of the gospel on a massive scale throughout our land. Now it is our decision whether we want to cover up our past or, following Josiah's example, allow the truth to penetrate our lives so that we can experience real healing in our land. (See 2 Kings 22.)

This is my hope, a healing hope: that this book might be one small part of that process of reconciling people together through the real searching of our souls.

John Perkins

Acknowledgments

Without the help, prayers and encouragement of many people, this book would have been impossible. I wish to express special thanks to Coleman Coates for the massive research he undertook for this book, to H. P. Spees for working so hard with me on the entire project, and to Earl Roe for his excellent editorial assistance in producing this book.

My acknowledgments go also—

To Momma Elizabeth and Papa James Wilson, who have shared the burden with me and who have given me great encouragement.

To Mr. Wayne Leitch who gave me a knowledge of the central truths of Scripture, the central truth upon which I was able to build my life and my ministry.

To Dr. Jack MacArthur and the fine congregation that he pastored; to the whole congregation of Calvary Bible Church, which was the first group of people to support the Voice of Calvary ministries.

To Frank Parker, James Robinson, Constance Slaughter, Larry Ross and all those brave civil rights lawyers who risked so much for so many people.

To Mr. and Mrs. R. A. Buckley, Jim Winston, Rev. Curry Brown, Rev. Calvin Bourne, Rev. James Howard and Rev. George Moore, who have been so unselfishly committed to me and to our ministry.

To Charlotte Graham and Lowell Noble, who so generously helped pull together many of the details for this classic edition.

To all my many friends around the country without whom there would be no story to tell, and no ministry to share.

My heartfelt thanks to each one of you.

Clyde

I remember when it happened like it was yesterday. Only it wasn't yesterday. It was summer 1946. The war was over, and it was cotton-picking time again in New Hebron.

That summer of 1946 was a hot one. Real hot—with a limp kind of heat that lay over the land like a blanket.

And that was when it happened.

White folks in New Hebron always said they weren't rich. And from their viewpoint, they were right. Only a couple of businessmen there were really well-off.

You know, this area in south-central Mississippi wasn't settled heavy until after 1800. So we didn't have the huge plantations like they show in those old antebellum movies. This wasn't rich bottomland, only rolling hills with small farms and smaller plantations.

These white folks—children and grandchildren, maybe, of some of those large plantation owners—filtered up this way from the delta or coast into our piney woods region. They moved in here, cleared the land and settled. Then they looked for sharecroppers to work full-time on the land, pick cotton for pennies a day and then pay back half their crops for rent.

Though they were a heap better off than the blacks, the way of life of local whites was modest enough that any change in the way things were was a personal threat to them. And in those days, keeping things the way they were meant keeping the blacks in line.

In fact, while the war was going on, a young black soldier, a sergeant, returned home to New Hebron on furlough. He was in town one day, wearing his uniform, stripes and all. But he got to drinking pretty heavy—to celebrate his leave at home, I guess.

A group of white men decided the sergeant had got too many big ideas. So they got hold of him and beat him almost to death with an ax handle. It happened on a Saturday.

Things like that made some black folks just move out. They left Mississippi—most of them for good—and headed north or west.

So like I said, things were a little bit different in 1946. Old King Cotton was tottering on the throne and his reign in the postwar South was shaky. There was no denying changes had come—the kind of changes that bother anybody, black or white, who likes things just to go along the same old way as before.

But lots of people had moved; whites and blacks alike had seen the rest of the country, the rest of the world. Some had, that is.

Actually, only one person in our family had escaped the rut of life in Mississippi, my brother Clyde. He was a dozen years older than me, but we were still real close. He was like a second father to me. Clyde was one who always stood up for himself. And that was true even before he got shipped off to Germany during the war—through no choice of his own. In World War II, all-white draft boards discovered in their newfound authority ways of getting "trouble-makin' niggers" out of town. And because of an incident a few years before, our local board had decided that Clyde was one such nigger.

On that earlier occasion, Clyde had gotten into an argument with a white man. And that wasn't safe, no matter how right you thought you were. Clyde committed the unpardonable sin of challenging The Man's absolute rightness.

"I want to see you dead" were the white man's parting words to Clyde.

Not long afterward, my brother was drafted and sent overseas.

Clyde did all right for himself in service. He was wounded several times in Germany. He returned home with combat ribbons, a Purple Heart, an honorable discharge—and a new attitude about the white man in Mississippi. Clyde was determined not to be pushed around anymore. He was a hero to all us kids; we used to follow him through town and marvel at his daring.

That white man did all right, too. While Clyde was away in the army, that man, DeWitt Armstrong, had been elected mayor of New Hebron. And the mayor's word always carried a lot of weight with the town marshal and his deputy.

It happened on a Saturday too, I remember.

You see, on Saturdays everyone would come up from the fields or wherever at noon. They stopped working for the day, washed up and all, and from about two o'clock on, folks would be coming into town to visit or just look around. Some would come into town in cars—or trucks, maybe—but others would drive in on mule wagons and tie up behind the stores.

Yes, people did travel some then, but town was the real center of life—and you either made it there or you didn't make it at all. So on that Saturday—or any Saturday, for that matter—everybody who could headed for Main Street.

Big, wide and paved, New Hebron's Main Street ran down a gentle slope from the dirt road at the upper edge of town to the railroad tracks of the lower end. Roads generally weren't so good in those days, so the railroad was really important to the community. It brought in dry goods, fertilizer, everything, and took out pulpwood and cotton from the gin at the lower end of town.

All the stores in town were one-story places, except Riley's General Merchandise, the largest business house in town.

Riley's was a two-story brick building with the main selling area on the ground floor, a second-level balcony above and a center space high and free between white pillars.

In town, groups of blacks, mostly sharecroppers and their families, drifted back and forth across Main Street or strolled along the sidewalks, stopping occasionally in the humid heat to mop their brows. Others sat around, fanning themselves and talking—mostly about the changes wrought by the far-off war, changes reflected in the wariness, the tension that was always there just under the surface on those crowded Saturday afternoons.

With all the black folks in town, the town's white marshal would be there, too, on the lookout for trouble, even when things were quiet. Self-consciously visible, he would walk along with the crowd making sure everyone knew he was there. He would peer into the faces of each group of blacks, making sure that no one was drunk or boisterous, that everyone was talking low and quiet-like.

Here on Main Street, a quick, almost casual swipe of the nightstick was a standard reminder of who was boss in New Hebron. So, when in town, blacks had to weigh every word and action. Young blacks especially, even without any particular grudge, could run afoul of the law in the most ordinary situations. And after 8:30 or so in the evening, blacks standing around on the street were not appreciated at all.

It was Saturday evening when it happened.

Along about sundown most of the farm families, black and white, started heading for home. Main Street began thinning of its parked cars and trucks. People who had come by wagon went around behind the row of stores to untie their mules and start on back home.

As the sun set and the families cleared out, most of the stores began closing up. Main Street grew quiet, as the heat thickened with dusk. Town people and the few others who still hung around were mostly in the one-block area where there were a couple of cafes, drug stores and Carolyn's Theater.

I was 16 that year and staying in town myself. So that Saturday night I was visiting at Charlie Wilson's place, a house that also had a little store in the front room, just sitting there and talking with friends. Clyde was over on Main Street about five, six blocks away, standing by Carolyn's Theater with his girl, Elma.

At the front of Carolyn's Theater, flanked by a cafe and a barber shop, were big glass double doors. Whites used this entrance.

To the left of the theater, between it and the five-and-dime next door, was a narrow alley leading to a side door with its own ticket booth. Blacks used this entrance. And stairs inside led to the theater balcony where blacks sat.

Clyde and Elma stepped into the alley and stood there talking. The alley was hot and already crowded. Since they hadn't opened up the ticket booth yet, the people were getting restless, and there was some pushing and shoving. So Clyde and Elma stayed at the back of the crowd, still talking.

Nobody's real sure just what started it all. But some folks say Clyde was talking loud, maybe even arguing with Elma about something. Anyway, a deputy marshal standing on the sidewalk yelled at them, "You niggers quiet down."

Clyde had been facing away from the sidewalk where the marshal stood. And as he turned to ask the marshal a question, the deputy clubbed him. Clyde got mad and, in self-defense, grabbed the marshal's club to keep the man from hitting him again. He struggled with the marshal.

That did it! The law now had all the excuse it needed. The marshal turned red in the face. You could see his eyes flash fire. He was so mad, he shook. And before anybody knew what was happening, he stepped back two steps, pulled out a gun and shot Clyde. Twice. In the stomach.

As soon as the marshal left, a crowd of blacks surrounded Clyde. One ran for a doctor. They picked Clyde up—he was still conscious—and carried him across the street to Seay's Drug Store, which had a doctor's office in the back. Whites could walk in through the front; blacks had to go around the building to the rear entrance.

I had just left Wilson's house and was getting into a car with some friends to go to Georgetown when another car came peeling up in the dust. "Clyde's been shot!" somebody yelled from the window of the car.

I just tore out of that place with the others. We piled into another car and roared off toward Main Street. I didn't know any details yet, but I was sure it was a white man that had shot Clyde, and that churned me up. Anger it was, not fear. I wasn't the least bit afraid for myself—just felt that churning fury inside that we ought to do something. We *had* to get even.

We turned onto Main Street and headed straight for Seay's. A bunch of people had already crowded into the doctor's office. By the time I managed to push my way into the room, they already had Clyde on the examining table. Words buzzed around—"the marshal shot him."

Doctor Langston, the town's two lawmen and one other white man were the only whites in that room full of black faces and black voices. That fourth white man was off to the side, but I could see he was bringing in an extra gun and ammunition for the marshal. He said a few words to the marshal. I tried hard to hear, but the noise of angry voices in the room, mixing in with the sound of the larger crowd outside the windows, covered up their words. I didn't need to hear the words. With a heaviness like steel in my stomach, I knew right then if I had a gun, I'd have shot that marshal.

Black faces watched the doctor, watched the marshal. And the marshal just stood there watching all of them—just "doin' his job."

As more people jammed into the office, I went to the head of the table. The doctor was leaning over Clyde, working on his wounds. I stood at Clyde's head, sometimes putting my hand on his cheek and mumbling to him. "Brother, don't die," I begged.

Doctor Langston looked up. "You have to get him to the hospital. I can't do anything more for him here."

We passed the word through the crowd and soon my cousin, Joe David, had his '41 Chevy at the back door. We carefully placed Clyde in the back seat. Then I and my Uncle Bill got in with him. Two others crowded in front with Joe, and we headed off into the night.

Jackson, the state capital and the nearest hospital, was an hour and a half or so away. The road was gravel from New Hebron north to Mendenhall; then we hit paved Route 49 into Jackson.

As the car sped on, life slowly slipped away from Clyde. He lay stretched out in the back, his head in my arms, oozing blood and dying by the inches. How? Why? I kept asking myself questions, even though I knew the answers didn't matter much anymore.

Clyde had to live. That was the only important thing now. But all we could do was keep on driving.

The miles stretched by in the night—past the white folks' houses, past the sharecroppers' shacks, past the cotton fields, past the tall stands of pine out there in the blackness.

At last—Jackson. We reached the hospital and got Clyde into a treatment room. Then there wasn't anything I could do but wait. Other carloads of blacks from New Hebron began to arrive. They waited, too.

I don't really remember much else about that night. But I do remember going into the room with Clyde for a few minutes. Something like a blood-pressure strap was on his arm.

A white man was there in the room. A doctor? Attendant? Someone waiting for a doctor? I don't know. He was just sitting there.

Later—how long I don't know—some other white person came out to the waiting room with the word. Clyde was dead!

Dead! My brother dead. All that army stuff about making the world safe for democracy. All that fighting some place off in Europe didn't get him killed. He had come home safe from the white man's war only to be shot down six months later by a white man in his own hometown.

The anger I first felt turned to a sort of blankness. I don't remember ever leaving the hospital. I don't remember going home. I don't remember the wake or anything else until the funeral.

Black folks came from all around and climbed to the hilltop four miles outside of town for the graveside ceremony in the cemetery of the Oak Ridge Baptist Church. Truth is, my family wasn't known for being church-going people. So the man who said a few words at the graveside was the undertaker, not a preacher. But it made no difference to me who said the words or what they were. I wasn't listening.

I saw the blue coffin lying open on the red earth. But the person inside didn't look a whole lot like Clyde anymore. The undertaker's efforts had not prevented the body from swelling and puffing.

Then the words were spoken and over. They closed the coffin and lowered it, and the folks began heading back to their homes.

It was all over. There was nothing more to be said about it. And there'd be no such thing as an official inquiry. If any whites stopped to think at all about my brother's death, they quite naturally took it for granted that whites in authority were always justified no matter what they did. No questions need ever be asked.

Black folks, too, from different motives, joined in the silence. With some the reason for sealed lips was obvious—they were practical enough to know where the power lay. In the case of Clyde's death, the way this worked out was simple: He was dead, and the others were safer if they said nothing about it.

But other blacks just didn't want to talk, and it wasn't just a matter of fear. It's hard to describe, really, but when you've spent your whole lifetime with limited opportunities, spent your whole lifetime being told your place is at the bottom—that entire mixture helps create a low image of yourself.

After a while, assertiveness or anger or whatever it's called just sort of dries up, like a muscle that never gets used. Some blacks were more like that than others. I wasn't, but if I'd drift over to a bunch of black folks sitting around talking, and if someone mentioned the incident, some might just sort of walk away. They'd just disconnect themselves. Clyde was dead, and that was that.

I stayed around New Hebron for a few more months. But several relatives felt that some of the family ought to leave town. Clyde was not the only family member who was likely to stand up to a white man.

The Perkins family was one of the toughest families around. We were bootleggers and gamblers, known for fighting and carrying on. A Perkins wouldn't take nothing off nobody, especially Uncles Bill and Bud. They didn't care who they got into it with. So everybody was afraid of us—even some of the white folks.

None of us Perkins' really was the quiet type, I guess. And some of my cooler-headed uncles were real afraid that some of us younger kin might not live quietly with the fact of Clyde's death. Somebody might provoke something against the white power structure.

Several of the family left for California. I went up to Jackson for a while to live with my Aunt Lillie Mae David—Cousin Joe's mother. Everybody called her "Sister." She had quit bootlegging and running skin games for a time to open a rooming house for blacks working in defense industries.

Then Sister and Uncle Bud got enough money together to send me west. I had one change of clothes, a lunch packed by Sister and three dollars left over after buying my ticket for California.

I boarded the train in Jackson. It chugged down to New Orleans where I changed for another one heading west. I rode on through Texas, New Mexico, Arizona, Nevada, California! Mississippi was behind me. Forever, I told myself. The year was 1947.

Jap

That long train ride west gave me plenty of time for thinking—and remembering, too. Even at 16, a guy has a lot to remember. And a lot to forget.

When I was born in 1930, my momma, Maggie, had pellagra and was just too sick to nurse me. Pellagra is a painful disease caused by protein deficiency. It was supposed to be a thing of the past in Mississippi by 1930, but Momma had it bad. All she could do—I have been told—was lay there in that sharecropper's house up on a hill by the cotton fields and try to get over it as best she could.

Though none of us knew then what protein deficiency was, we sure knew that milk helped a whole lot. But nobody in our family, none of our relatives, owned a cow. And the plantation owner said there wasn't enough pasture for keeping cows, so none of his sharecroppers could have one.

Because Momma couldn't nurse me, I just lay there beside her, growing weak from hunger. But then my grandmother found a sharecropper on a nearby plantation who had a cow, and that neighbor offered to give us some of the milk for my feeding. So each day a little milk was brought over for me.

I lived, but seven months after I was born, Momma died. So, in a way, before I had any real consciousness of life, I had won my first battle with death. Looking back now, I know that God kept me then for His work. But it was many years before I thought much about God. My father, Jap, left home around the time Momma died. So Grandma—Jap's mother—took in all five of us Perkins kids—Clyde, Mary, Clifton, Imogene and me. Grandma Perkins—Aunt Babe Perkins to most everybody else around those parts—was a widow and had already raised 19 kids of her own. But she took us in and made a home for us anyway.

Eventually Aunt Babe had to give away three of us Perkins kids. But I was little, so she kept me. And Clyde was big enough to help with chores, so she kept him too. Aunt Babe lived on Mr. Fred Bush's place. And she stayed on Bush's place for maybe four, five years, from about the time I was three until I was seven. That's why the first thing I remember is living with my grandma on the Bush place.

Mr. Fred Bush. I remember that name well, because that name was just about the first words I had to learn—my first introduction to a segregated society. You see, who I was in those days was described only in terms of a dependent relationship to a white man.

Back then, if a black child was walking along the road or was in town on a Saturday, and he met an older white person, the white's first words would be, "What place you live on, boy?"

I had to know the answer. Because I wasn't anybody all by myself, or even by who my family was. I wasn't important in their eyes; only the person I was connected to. And it meant that my own name, John Perkins, had no significance; only the name of the man on whose land I lived. So right from the beginning, I learned the proper reply, "Mr. Bush's place," whenever someone asked me where I belonged.

Our own house on Bush's place had three rooms and a kitchen. With a couple of aunts, uncles and some cousins living there, too, our family varied between 12 and 15 people all the time. There were only five beds. So we younger children had to sleep head to foot in a bed—several at the head and some more at the foot—eight of us together on a shuck bed.

Breakfast at Grandma's place was plain—flour gravy and corn bread. Grandma would heat up flour in a skillet with a dab of lard and brown it a bit for flavor. Then she would add water to make the gravy. Sometimes she had a piece of pork or salt back to add to it.

Lunch would be simple, especially when we'd be in school and have to take something with us—usually a bit of corn bread or some biscuits with homemade jelly.

Grandma's cabin stood on flat ground almost within sight of town. The house backed onto a stretch of woods—mostly pine with some oaks. And in front of the house, cotton fields stretched most of the way to New Hebron, a couple of miles away.

Close by the house, a stream had cut a deep channel between the woods and the fields that led up to Mr. Bush's house. The Illinois Central Railroad tracks bridged the stream at a spot where we used to play and swim a lot.

At noontime on days when the heat stood still over the fields, we kids would bring the mules down to the stream where they could drink and rest in the shade of some of those tall oaks. Then we'd head upstream a bit where there was a real deep swimming hole, or maybe play around the railroad trestle itself. I liked to climb up the slant of the braces, up onto the track and back down again.

Growing up in a family with a bunch of cousins can be fun sometimes. But other times, it hurts a lot. For teasing, sometimes even cruel teasing, was a regular part of our life. Some of my cousins were born out of wedlock, but they at least had their mothers with them. I didn't. My momma was dead, and in that whole collection of relatives, there was no one who really belonged to me.

That's why one thing at Bush's place sticks most in my mind. It comes back again and again as a scene that sort of wraps up all the longings, the fears, the inside stirring up that made me always reach out for something solid, something real—just for me.

It was the time I first remember seeing my father, Jap. I don't know how old I was then, four maybe. But it was about the very first real event I can remember.

It's rather hard to explain now just how important it was for me to see my daddy and have him with me. You see, this was the deep South during the Depression. Economic hardship and despair pretty much dominated all of life in the black community.

It was a tough life. And families struggled for existence. But somehow we endured.

And like I said, teasing in the black community can be cruel and direct and strong. So if a kid doesn't have a father, he is a bastard and is open to any sort of teasing that might come his way.

But I wasn't a bastard! I had a father, and I knew it. My aunts and grandmother told me so. And my father *had been married* to my mother. He may not have lived at home, but he was my father. He was *mine!* Nobody else's but *mine!*

And then, all of a sudden, Jap was home. My daddy was home. He came up on a visit from Columbia, Mississippi, where he had been living, and stayed with us overnight. He arrived late one Friday night after I had fallen asleep—alone in a crowded house. He woke me up, and I saw him in the glow of the lamp. There was love in his face. Love for me.

He hugged me in strong arms. And he talked to me. My daddy! It was the first time someone loved me just for myself.

It was a wonder I slept at all that night. For the joy of belonging, of being loved, was almost more than my heart could hold.

And I could hardly wait for morning to proudly show off my daddy—not my "Uncle Jap"—to all those kids who had teased me about him.

You see, that teasing I talked about, about fathers, I understood it enough even at my age, to call him "Daddy" instead of "Uncle"—the usual term kids had to use for the man they resembled and who occasionally showed up with their mothers.

This man was my daddy. And I could prove it. I slept content.

I remember the feelings more than the events of the next morning. Again Daddy talked to me, showed special love to me. I almost forgot to mind his calling me "Baby"—what with me being his youngest and all. I was just that happy to be with him again—to see him and to touch him.

So when he said he would be going into New Hebron with the regular Saturday afternoon crowd to catch a ride back to Columbia again, there was only one thing on my mind: *I would go with him!*

Now, you see, this was not the kind of wish where you just *choose* something, like vanilla instead of chocolate ice cream. It was more than a wish; it was a deep-down feeling inside that we should, we would, both go away together.

Naturally, we would both go. No question about it. After all, he was my daddy. Not just the man who fathered me, but my daddy. My family!

It was just after noontime on Saturday when Daddy started down the lane by the railroad tracks where we ran the cows. I saw he was heading toward town and started following him.

"Daddy!"

Jap turned and saw me following.

"Go back. Go back."

The way he ordered me back sounded strange, like he was confused somewhat. Yet he didn't really sound like he was angry with me, so I followed, but at a careful distance behind.

I wondered what was wrong. I knew my daddy loved me. So why didn't he want me to go with him?

As the lane ran out, Daddy moved up onto the railroad tracks. I trailed him. And when he stopped, I stopped. When he moved on, I followed.

He knew I was still there behind him, because he came back—a couple of times, I think—and whupped me with a switch from a tree. After that, I gauged my distance better—far enough back to run if he came toward me, but close enough to see him through my tears, and keep following him.

I was so mixed up, I didn't know what to think. Why was Daddy punishing me? I hadn't done anything wrong. I only wanted to go with him. That's all I wanted. And I wanted it more than anything else in the world. Even when *he* switched me, I sensed that Daddy wasn't really mad at me. He just seemed worried, real worried. And it wasn't just because I was up there on the tracks. After all, he was right there with me.

My heart was breaking. Why couldn't Daddy tell I just wanted to go with him? I was afraid, terribly afraid if he got out of sight, I would never see him anymore.

"Daddy! Please, Daddy! Take me with you. Don't leave me alone again."

Jap stopped and looked back at me once more. That strange, sad look was still on his face. I reached toward him and wanted to run to him. But I was afraid. He still held that switch in his hand. I could only stand there and cry.

I knew then that Daddy was going away without me. But I still didn't turn back. So once more he came back and whupped me a last time.

Just then my Auntie came up. She must have missed me and followed after me. I stood there between the two of them, neither one saying anything. Then she took me by the hand and dragged me away, back down the tracks toward home.

I looked back once, but Daddy was already gone. And with him went my newfound joy in belonging, in being loved, in being somebody for just a little while. Years would pass before I would know this joy again.

I cried all the way back to the house, holding tightly to Auntie with one hand and carrying my heart with the other.

What was Daddy really thinking, what was in his mind that day he left me? I never found out. I never ever really had a chance to talk with Jap in the few times I saw him again before he died.

But I do know that, even when he punished me for following him that afternoon, he was admitting we had some sort of *relationship*. And that need for relationship was a weight I carried, a need that remained unmet for me much of the rest of my life.

Learning to Survive

The higher ground of the plantation beyond the stream led to the big house of Mr. Fred Bush. Mr. Bush had been a lawyer, but while still young had lost his hearing. Still he could make a good life for himself here on the plantation. It was the sort of life where, for a white man, hearing mattered less than talking.

Up by the big house were small houses for house servants. Naturally these servants were selected from among those blacks who were most agreeable to the white world. So they were not always liked or trusted by other blacks.

The house servants did no sharecropping. The women of the two- or three-servant households on the plantation worked as cooks, maids, nursemaids. Their men did various lifting chores too heavy for the maids, kept up supplies of firewood for the cooks, fixed fences and tended the buildings.

Among the sharecroppers on the Bush place, each household was responsible for its own fields. But in the spring, we broke the land together, with Mr. Bush deciding whose fields would be plowed first.

Though my family was all sharecroppers until I left for California in 1947, this was the last really big plantation I lived on. After my grandmother and aunts moved from the Fred Bush place, they always lived on smaller farms where their household was either the only one or else the main sharecropping household on the property.

Yet my family had other things to do beside sharecropping. All of us, or most—my grandmother, aunts, some uncles—made some extra money in gambling. But because Mississippi was officially dry—remaining that way until the '60s—we made our real money in bootlegging.

And bootlegging was why our family moved to small places, where we would be less burdened with large farm projects. And we kept as close to town as we could, so our moonshine business would grow. You see, most of our daytime, weekday sales were to whites who would drive up and buy a pint or two.

One of my uncles was a wholesale bootleg distributor. He would take his pickup down Biloxi way or down the coast toward Picayune for a load of moonshine. That was a good area for bootlegging—stills could be easily hid in the swamps. There were some stills in the woods closer to home, of course, like in Rankin County, east of Jackson. But the people who really liked moonshine always said the coast whiskey was best.

Distributors would sell moonshine by the gallon or keg— 10, 25, sometimes 50 gallons at $3 to $4 a gallon. The retailers would sell it for about a dollar a half-pint, taking in $16 a gallon. One of my aunts—Aunt Coot—was a really big retailer. Her business was so good she added another line for the weekends when she had most of her black customers: gambling.

Sharecropping made it easier for us to run our illegal businesses. But don't think we only pretended to be sharecroppers. Sharecropping was a lot more than just a cover for our various activities—it was real work, hard work all those years.

White attitudes made sharecropping a necessity for most blacks. For, as sharecroppers, we lived the proper role and behaved in the accepted manner. Sharecroppers weren't considered dangerous types who might upset the system. So our family's status as sharecroppers provided a stability of sorts not always open to independent blacks.

Trying to be an independent black in the postwar South could be risky. We could have been put out of business if we had tried to go it on our own, totally independent. That would have been "uppity."

You see, prejudice in the South is both paternalistic and antagonistic. What most Southern whites want is for blacks to be part of the Southern system, to have a "proper" relationship to the white Establishment. That's why independence for a black in the South is a worse crime than merely being illegal. And that's why independent black farmers—small farm owners—had such a difficult time making it on their own without the help of those with the resources.

In this system of paternalism, a white developed a sort of feeling of ownership in his relationship to his sharecroppers or employees. So strong was this attitude that no one, not even a law officer, who had business with a sharecropper, would go directly to him without the permission or understanding of the white landowner. Disturbing a sharecropper could be interpreted as disturbing his boss.

Of course, every now and then the law would come our way. So we had to be careful all right. But with us youngsters, those raids by the lawmen were almost a joke. It was a good time for us to put one over on the white system.

In those early days, bootlegging was no big deal. It was big business all right, but all the sheriffs had bootleggers, too. So bootleggers were somewhat accepted, if you had the right relationship with the right people.

It was only during Prohibition when the internal revenue people came in and overrode the local establishment that bootlegging was brought under control. And then the sheriffs themselves began enforcing the law.

But cars traveling over dirt roads make plenty of noise. So we could always hear in plenty of time when the raiding party was coming. And we always had our own plans laid out in advance—just in case.

It wasn't easy for the sheriff to make a raid directly at the house while whiskey was being sold. The law, the rules of the game, said the actual whiskey had to be seized as evidence. So a room could smell powerfully of moonshine, but if no whiskey itself was found, there was not a drop of evidence for the sheriff to make a case.

Aunt Coot, being a big retailer, knew how to run her business. She knew pretty well just how much she'd need to keep on hand for any one day's business. So she bought only so much at a time from her distributor. And she always kept her cache of moonshine down in the woods behind the house, bringing up only one day's supply at a time in quart jars from her storage spots hidden in the woods. That way, if there was a raid, only that day's supply—and no more—would be lost when she emptied the jars in a hurry.

Our method of operation was simple. Anytime anyone drove up to the house, one of us would go to the room where the whiskey was kept and stay with it, ready to dump it, until the call came that the visitor was either a friend or a customer.

But this system worked only when the sheriff made a raid on the house. Sometimes he would try something else. He'd come up with his deputies and make a sweep through the woods, searching for Aunt Coot's hiding places. But again we were too quick, the woods too big and the raiders too few for these periodic sweeps to amount to anything.

In the woods we dug deep, narrow holes just big enough to hold a few quart jars stacked one on top of the other. Next we'd cover the hole with maybe a rotted pine stump just the right size and push the pine needles and leaves back around it. Then we kids would hide and watch the fun as the raiders searched the woods.

The sheriff's men went through the woods and swamps with big rubber hip boots and poles, poking around here and there, looking for our hidden whiskey. More often than not they'd dig up a real pine stump instead of the one hiding the whiskey. And then we kids, watching in silence from our own hiding places, would hug ourselves with glee over the frustrated efforts of the searchers.

Sometimes we put our holes right in the paths that ran through the woods from one plantation to another. Then we watched, pleased as could be, while all those lawmen walked up and down over the hidden moonshine. We'd almost have to fight ourselves not to giggle out loud when one of those hot, frustrated deputies would stop right on top of where we had hidden the whiskey. He'd stand there mopping his face and cussing to himself, while we liked to die with fits of laughing.

And it was almost more than we could stand when the lawmen would leave the path and spread out through the woods, searching so hard on each side of the trail where the treasure lay. Finally they'd leave, all tired and disgusted, and we kids would watch them go, able at last to laugh out loud in our latest victory over a system that—even as kids—we had already learned to fear and despise.

I remember when I was only nine or ten years old how a young black man accidentally ran over a white man uptown. The black was locked in jail. Later, white people came, took him out, tied him behind a car and dragged him up and down the streets of the town on a Saturday afternoon until he was dead.

I remember when it happened like it was yesterday. Because that young black got killed just like Clyde got killed. On Main Street. On Saturday.

By somebody white.

Farming on Halves

Like I said, even when bootlegging was going good, cotton was what set the basic pattern of our lives. The whole community centered on cotton. And my memories fit together that way. For instance, when I try to think back and remember, I say, "Well, we got in two crops at that one place, so we lived there two years." Or, "It was cotton-picking time when Clyde was killed." And only then do I remember the actual dates.

The cotton year began in January or February. Each sharecropper went up to the boss's house one at a time to make his "arrangements" for the coming year. If he had plans to move to another place, he would have to move then, because once he committed himself to another season, he'd be locked in till November at least.

February can be chilly in Mississippi. The fields are all dry and brown. Only the pines are still green. The early morning sun hasn't burnt off the frost when the sharecropper goes up to the white house. He walks fast to keep warm and heads, not for the front door, but for the back door. He knocks and—depending on what the weather is like and how the boss feels—maybe he is invited into the kitchen, the only part of a white man's house that many black field hands ever see.

But usually the two men talk outside. We called this procedure "the arrangement" or "furnishing." After a proper "Good morning" and all, the sharecropper might say, "Mr. Pierpoint, I'm here to make arrangements for crops this year."

And Mr. Pierpoint would ask, "Okay, Bill, what are you going to need?" Instead of using the worker's name, the boss man might use a favorite nickname: "Tupi," "Red," "Shorty," "Slim," or whatever. A person without a nickname was uncommon.

Sharecropper Bill would reply, "Oh, 10 dollars."

That was 10 dollars a month—about the highest amount paid during the '30s. Some smaller families might try to get by with three, though that would take a lot of extra work like hunting to keep food on the table.

Mr. Pierpoint scratches his head for a moment before replying. "Now, Bill, that's too much, that's too much. You can get by on less than 10 dollars."

Bill keeps at it. "But my wife had another baby."

The Man still isn't convinced. "Well, yeah, but you can still get by on nine."

After a few more minutes of this sort of talk, they agree on an amount, and the boss says, "Well, you can do your trading at Mr. So-and-so's store."

Along with the talking about money, they agree on the number of acres of corn and cotton to plant.

Another crop year was on its way.

By the way, there was a reason for the boss saying where his sharecroppers could trade. Many small plantation owners wouldn't have enough cash themselves to furnish their sharecroppers before the crop came in. But they had a friend or a relative who owned a store. They would designate that store as the one where the sharecropper could get the amount of groceries monthly they had agreed upon. The landowner would be billed, not the sharecropper.

The storekeeper himself would charge about 25 percent interest, and the boss would add his own charges—sometimes another 20 percent. The landowner charged interest even though he was not directly loaning the money out of his pocket, because he was the one being billed. He was the one "standing for" his sharecroppers.

So the sharecropper paid between 35 percent and 45 percent interest on the crop loan. That interest, plus principal, he had to pay out of his share of the crops. And his share was only half; the other half belonged to the landowner. That's what people meant when they said we "farmed on halves."

The first task in February was to clear the land of dead brush and weeds. For a while, when I was nine, I had my own extra job for money, feeding chickens for a nearby white woman. I'd do that early, so I could join my cousins and Clyde and an uncle or two for land-clearing. The older ones would do the heavy work, cutting with hoes and axes. We younger kids would pile up the cuttings.

Before February was over, it was time to start breaking up the land. Many boys as young as 10 had to do their own small share of plowing, but by the time I was that old, Aunt Coot, who took me in after my grandmother died, was only living on small places. So my uncles handled all the plowing.

Though the family bootlegging may have made things a little easier for us compared with some of the really struggling families, I was always working, long and hard. I guess the biggest difference our bootlegging business made in my life was in the attitudes it created, rather than in any real money then and there.

Like all the Perkins family, I was a merchant. I learned the idea—and meaning of the word—at an early age. Always looking for the opportunity. And that meant more than just getting things; it meant having a bit of confidence in myself that things could be done. Done for myself, of course, because I was very selfish. But done.

All this sort of stayed with me under the surface even in those early years when an outsider wouldn't really have thought our family looked any better off than lots of other sharecroppers around. Same cramped house, same hard field work, nothing special that showed. Like all blacks, we had no electricity; we just used pine splinters or kerosene lamps.

Even when the first electric lines came into the area in the late '30s, they were strictly for whites. But Aunt Coot, in her usual way, reaped some benefit from that event. She took in as boarders some of the black laborers for the several months they were around putting in the lines. But not until I left for California in 1947 did my family have electricity.

We'd continue the plowing through February. Early March was corn-planting time, and then cotton at the end of March into early April. I'd be out every day on all the jobs, like putting fertilizer into the furrows by handfuls.

With the corn and cotton planted, we could then put in a few vegetable patches for our own use—peas, watermelon, peanuts, and maybe a few other things. These foodstuffs were really important, because the monthly furnishing arrangement with the boss did not continue clear up to cotton harvest time. Sharecroppers had to make it on their own from late summer until the final settling of the cotton crop.

That's the way each year went: moving from one thing to another. After we planted our vegetable patches, it would be time to thin out the corn. Next the corn would have to be chopped free of weeds. Then one more round of fertilizer for the corn, called "side dressing." Even though cotton was planted later than corn, it came up quickly, as soon as eight or ten days after planting. So from then on, we were always chopping cotton.

I don't ever remember having spare time or an easy time but I'm sure there must have been some difference between our own hard work and the way some families would be totally exhausted or wiped out by emergencies—families that didn't have our kind of extra income.

Corn and cotton then were the main jobs through the summer. Peas came up quickly—around May. Other vegetables were up later and we'd can some, as well as eating fresh. When I could, I'd go out berry picking with my cousins.

Cotton harvest could last a long time. Sometimes the first cotton would be ready by late August, but picking would continue through October. Cotton-picking time was one time it was good to have a large family. Some families might try to pick one bale a day, though that was top speed for a good-size group. We might pick only two bales a week. A bale is 1,200 pounds.

At the edge of the larger fields was a shed, a cotton house. Up high near the door was an arm of wood to hang a scale on. We'd pick our way toward the cotton house, weigh the full sack and empty it.

If we did real good during the morning or had some cotton left from the day before, we'd get over 600 pounds by noon. Then we'd break for lunch and bring the mules and wagon up to the field. All during the blazing hot afternoon we'd pick, weigh, and then dump our sacks directly into the wagon. Then at the end of the day, we'd add the cotton that was already piled in the shed.

With our wagon full, we'd climb in and head for the cotton gin in town. And we'd be tired, real tired. But some nights after supper, maybe, we'd go back into the fields again and pick more cotton by moonlight.

Field corn would be harvested well into November, and then another crop year was over. We and all the other sharecroppers would settle our accounts with the boss man and then hope for a better crop next year.

Not all blacks picking cotton and corn were sharecroppers. Some—like the small-farm owners—also picked cotton to earn extra money. After they'd get through picking their own crops, they'd hire themselves out as hands and pick cotton on other farms. They'd go from place to place—sometimes as far as the delta—riding in the back of big, roofless trucks like so many animals going to market.

Those hired workers really had it rough. On the job, they'd stay in old, dilapidated, rat-infested shacks on some planter's place and get groceries on credit at the local store—also owned by the planter.

Hired workers slept on the floor on mattresses they made themselves with cotton they picked after getting hired. And they brought their own quilts with them when they came; otherwise there was nothing to cover up with at night. There were no lights, water or gas, of course. But if they were lucky, they might have a two-burner oil stove to fry their food on. Yet there was nothing they had that would fight off the chill of those early mornings and late nights.

Hired pickers got something like $2.00 or $2.50 per 100 pounds at the beginning of the season. This was because the new, fresh-opened cotton was still thick and heavy. So by 10 o'clock in the morning, a good picker might already have 100 to 150 pounds—two sacks full. Every picker—sharecropper or hired— dragged a nine-foot sack while he worked. And when that sack was full, a worker knew he had 75 pounds of cotton in it.

Those were days we'd all like to forget. But conditions in the cotton fields were still pretty much the same when I finally went west in 1947. And they didn't change much after that till around 1950 or '51 when the plantation owners started putting those big mechanized cotton pickers into the fields. That put a lot of folks out of work. And since most blacks couldn't get any poorer than they were and still survive, lots of them went north. Those who remained became almost destitute. This condition continues most everywhere in Mississippi today, except in places, say, like Simpson County where a factory or two has moved in and made a few jobs for people. But things still haven't changed all that much for the poor anywhere in Mississippi.

At least, not yet.

Challenging the System

Anyway, like I said, we sharecroppers lived from one crop year to the next. And only when the crop year ended did school begin. Naturally, school couldn't interfere with farming. Since share-croppers needed to be in the fields until all the crops were in, their kids didn't start school until late November or December.

And since land clearing always began in early February, that meant that school for sharecroppers was only about three months a year: November, December and January. With such a short school year, there was no such thing as finishing one grade a year; it was more like one grade level every two years or so.

Our teachers usually came from outside the community, living-in only for the brief school year. An eighth-grade graduate could teach, but high school graduates were preferred.

During my first year of school, I was still living at Grandma's place—the same place where I had first seen my father. We never lived real close to any school, so going to school sure didn't get much encouragement from our family. And I don't remember anyone in our home ever getting excited about what school might do for me.

I was six when I started at Greenwood Elementary School. It was all black, all eight grades together. My first day of school I ate breakfast with my cousins, then wrapped up my lunch of biscuits and jam and headed off with the group.

That afternoon I brought home a note from my teacher. I needed a book. A book! Now that was some kind of event.

My Aunt Ethel took me to town. We went into the drugstore. She put down 20 cents on the counter, and I reached for that new thing that was mine. Now I could learn to read!

We had the usual three Rs in school. And sometimes a teacher would throw in an extra like geography or health. But school health didn't have a whole lot to do with our own health; the advice wasn't all that practical. I can still remember a teacher's solemn instructions on tooth brushing when no one I knew owned a toothbrush.

I loved basketball and baseball, which were always good reasons for going to school. And some of us boys made little carts with wheels we sawed off of sweetgum logs. We'd climb on these things and go whooshing down the steep ravine behind the school. Getting banged up now and then only added to the thrill.

One school I went to was pretty large for a rural school, with close to 200 students. Since school was only in winter, I always think of being cold when I think of school. We had stoves in the middle of each room, but some days if it was too cold or if there wasn't enough wood, they'd just dismiss school.

Firewood—and most everything else—had to be provided through the local community and PTA, since only teachers' salaries were paid by the county. There were separate school boards for black and white schools up into the late '50s. Since the black school boards had less money, they couldn't provide things like school buses.

Every day on the highway about the black section of town, big, beautiful, yellow school buses brought in the white students from their homes to their elementary schools. Since there were no school buses for black students, the black elementary students walked—and dodged spitballs thrown from the windows of the buses that passed them.

Few black rural Mississippians went on to high school at that time, so high schools for them were few and far between. Black high school students not fortunate enough to live near one of their own schools often had to find room and board away from home during the week.

I think I reached about the fifth-grade level when I finally quit going to school for good. That was around 1945, and I was 15 then. You see, I quit school twice: the first time in 1942 when I was about 12. I stayed out a couple of years and didn't go back until sometime in 1944. Then I came back for one more year.

Actually, in that last year I didn't come to learn, but to play ball. I might be in school one or two days a week. But, like I said, it didn't matter much to my family either way. So I really had no one to encourage me to stay in school.

But even as a school kid, I was already learning my most important lessons in life outside the classroom. In fact, I was only a boy about 11 or 12 when I got my first lesson in economics. And I learned that one on the job.

I was away from home at the time. To go away from home back then was to go 12 or 14 miles away from where a person lived. So I was away from home one summer visiting this friend of mine. A white man from a plantation in the area was busy hauling hay. And the man was in a hurry to get that hay inside quickly before it rained. This man needed somebody to help him haul hay, and I needed some money. So I figured this was a good chance to work for the day and maybe make a dollar and a half or two dollars. At least that was what they were paying for a day's work, and that's what I expected to get.

I went to work for that man, and I worked all day. At the end of the day, he gave me 15 cents! I could hardly believe it. Fifteen cents!

I had earned it, but I didn't know whether to take the money or not. Here was a white man handing it to me. I was in his house. And I had worked for him.

But I was afraid. Afraid if I accepted the money, I would hate myself for taking it. Afraid too if I didn't take the money, the man would say I was an "uppity, bigoted nigger" or maybe a "smart nigger." And at that time in Mississippi, it was tough enough just being black; to be known as a smart nigger would have been unbearable.

Twelve years old. Alone. My first time going out on my own in the workaday world. My first confrontation with a white employer. My first face-to-face encounter with "the system." I took the 15 cents. A dime and a buffalo nickel. And I couldn't do a thing.

But I went away from there asking myself some questions: What happened to me? How was this white man able to exploit me?

I took a long look at what had just happened to me and really began thinking about economics. That man had the capital: the land and the hay. And he had the means of production: the wagon and the horses. All I had were my wants and needs—and my labor. So I was exploited. I told myself, "Tupy, this system is a system of capital. Get capital, control it and know how to use it.

"And if you're going to make it in this society, you've got to somehow or other get your hands on the means of production. Once you get the means of production, you can do good or evil with it. And this man done evil with it. He exploited you."

Yes, at a very early age I learned that. And from that day on I began to understand something about the economic system and how it worked.

By the time I was 13, I felt I was a man. I was making my own decisions, such as which aunt or cousin was the best one to live with. I realize a lot of this was my heritage from my grandmother, a really strong-willed woman and, in her way, an intelligent, self-confident person. Grandma had no fear, no fear at all of white people.

So I guess it wasn't too unusual that I made my first challenge to the system when I was just 14. With my cousin Jimmy, I went looking for some extra cash work besides the chores I had to do at home. We contracted to cut some heavy bushes and undergrowth from a pasture owned by a white farmer.

Most people thought of this man as fair-minded—at least by local standards. He always gave those who worked for him a good meal. So we agreed to work for a gallon of syrup and a meal per day.

We went to work, and it was tough going. But we worked hard and steady all morning. Then when lunch time came, we went around to the kitchen for our food.

Well, the farmer's mother-in-law was staying with them for a long visit. She met us at the back door, and no way was she about to be helpful. Instead of giving us the meal we had agreed on, she handed us trimmings and scraps off their table. Then she closed the door.

Jimmy and I looked at our plates and then looked at each other. Who could work all day on a handful of leavings? We decided we couldn't and went home, leaving the job and the tools.

When her son-in-law heard what we did, he got real upset and came over to our place. He asked us to come back and finish the job. And he promised that we could eat at his mother's house, not too far away.

We agreed and went back to work. But that incident always stuck in my mind. It was my first small push for justice through economic pressure.

My becoming more and more independent eventually led to my first real trip away from home. I had heard that my father was still living in Columbia. So I went south to visit him for a while.

But Columbia wasn't a very easy place to be, since the woman Jap was living with didn't like me at all. Not one bit. Still, that didn't stop me from wanting to stay on as long as I could.

Finally Aunt Coot, always the active one, found a job for me. She came down to Columbia and persuaded me to return to New Hebron. So I went back and took the job. But I hated it. I really did.

I had done small cash jobs for whites before, but this was my first time of working for a monthly salary under direct supervision of whites. In all the years of hard times we had gone through, my work was mostly with our own family, sharecropping or helping with the bootlegging business. So what we did was always our own concern, our own project.

But this time it was different. I still worked for a family. But it wasn't mine. And it wasn't black. Now I worked for the Smiths, a white family of unmarried sisters and a brother. They lived in one of the few old houses in our area built before the Civil War.

The pay was only $20 a month. I felt I should be getting more than that. But even for more money, I didn't want to keep on working there. I had promised Aunt Coot that I would, but I just knew I couldn't stay on much longer at the Smith place.

I didn't know it then, but a bigger change was in store for me—bigger than just another job. It was a whole lot bigger, because this was the summer of 1946—only a few weeks before my brother Clyde was killed!

And only a few months before I went west to California.

Who Needs Religion?

Ninety-eight cents an hour. That's what I got in 1947 on my first job in California at the Union Pacific Foundry in South Gate. And it sure sounded like good money to me. I could still taste the bitterness of that $20 a month back in Mississippi.

But money was only part of the good feeling I had. In Mississippi every move I made was defined in terms of my race. I worked on farms and fields, I behaved in certain ways toward my employers, and I received certain wages—all of this defined in terms of my blackness. And in every one of these areas there were different standards for whites.

But here in California I was getting the same wages as whites and working right along with them. Now, I've learned over the years that racism exists nationwide—yes, even outside the deep South. But socioeconomic structures in Northern urban areas maintain the ghettos and white supremacy in a mechanical way, so Northern whites have never had to be open, active racists as was true in the South.

All of that I would learn later. But right then, in Southern California, I could see glimpses of hope that were once blocked off to me. I could live now.

Clyde was dead, and so were old times back in Mississippi. Not one to look back, I pushed on in my new life. At the time, I was staying with a cousin in the town of Monrovia. And we drove 60 miles round trip together every day between Monrovia and South Gate.

1947 was a good year to get in on the action at the foundry. I was on the ground floor of a new operation in a plant that was joining in the postwar boom. I was part of a crew making cast-iron pipes for sewage and plumbing.

Our crew was actually part of the process of refining the system—shifting from a slow, individualized operation to a production line setup. I worked on every phase of the operation; and it took about a year to work out all the kinks. Under the old system, each crew would produce between 90 and 100 pipes a shift. But under the new system, with operations on a turntable, production went up into the thousands. We'd have eight or ten molds in different stages of production from sand to pouring iron, with the finished item finally pushed off onto a belt.

You can bet management was pleased—with increased production, that is, not with the stepped-up activity of union organizers in the plant. We got a few threats from management that those who voted for the union would be fired, but that didn't stop us from voting to join the United Steel Workers. I had already done a good job of helping to organize the production line, and that included managing men, too. So I became our department's union steward.

But as production increased, pay remained on the same hourly scale, and we all felt we deserved a bigger piece of the action. After all, we had helped devise the system that was bringing in that extra profit.

So I got right in the thick of organizing a strike that succeeded in bringing our workers a number of benefits, such as a piecework provision that sometimes brought me $100 a week—pretty good money for then. Even years later, with some of the other things I managed to do, I still look back to that event as my claim to fame: pulling that strike together. I never forgot the potency of united action.

All that, and I was not yet out of my teens.

In 1949, I went back to Mississippi on a visit. That was when I met Vera Mae Buckley again. I say again, because relatives say we played together as kids, but neither of us remembers that.

In fact, Vera Mae's first recollection of seeing me was at my sister's funeral when I was real young. My sister had been killed by her boyfriend. Vera remembered how sad it was, and when she got home after the funeral she asked her grandmother, "Who was that little boy standing under the tree in the middle of the graveyard and crying?"

"Oh, that was Tupy, one of the Perkins boys," her grandmother told her, using the nickname my family had given me. Then her grandmother went on to tell her a lot more about the Perkins family.

In those days, my people and Vera's people lived real close. In fact, Vera Mae's daddy and my daddy were great friends; they drank together.

Vera Mae had a good family background. Her family was among the few small farm owners in the area. And they were a church-going family, which made them just a bit suspicious of that no-church, bootlegging Perkins crowd.

So her family wasn't too sure a Perkins might be good for one of their girls when I began courting Vera Mae. They just didn't know then what plans God had up the road for both of us.

Vera Mae and I met one Sunday on the church grounds. And the way we met tells a lot about what the black church was like in the 1930s and '40s when I was growing up. In those days, there was no other place to go for social life but the church.

Church people, you see, couldn't go to the movies. People who did that weren't much different than outlaws, whoremongers and the like. And there were so few cars, we couldn't just run into Jackson when we wanted to. So most of the time, the church was where girls and boys met their future spouses.

Ever since slavery, the black church in the South served as the only place where black people could get together and speak freely. At such gatherings, there was always a lot of gambling and drinking in the woods nearby. A white law officer was always there, either to keep people from shooting each other or because he had a man of his own selling whiskey down in the woods, and he didn't want any competition.

Sometimes there were big meetings, like church revivals, where people from all over the town would come. And when we had Church Association Meetings, people from churches everywhere in the county and surrounding parts would come. They set up booths to sell every kinda food, chewing gum and candy. These booths were open all night long.

Fish sandwiches were a specialty. These were a production-line affair where the women would get these big pots used for boiling clothes and fill them full of hog fat. Then they'd cut these big buffalo fish into slabs, fry them in the fat and make them into sandwiches. They'd still be hot when you ate them.

Since this was in a time before there were a lot of cars, these meetings were about all the socializing there was to do— the only socializing that was acceptable, that is. So some people came to church not to worship, but to eat, court, drink and gamble. This type of meeting lasted until about the early 1950s in the South, until black people went north by the thousands. And with a lot more cars, mobility was a lot easier, and the meetings weren't needed too much anymore.

With all that action going on outside the church house, there wasn't too much going on inside. The men sat on one side of the church and the women on the other. The young people sat in the center. A lot of folks, especially the young people, could hardly wait till it was time for the collection.

When the preacher ended his sermon, the deacons got up and told everybody, "It's time to take the offering." The congregation began singing. Then starting from the back, the people would stand, march to the front, lay their money on a table and go back to their seats—only the young people marched right on outside. Some of the older ones went outside, too.

I was on the Pleasant Hill Baptist Church grounds when Vera Mae came out of the church that Sunday. Like most everybody else, I was there for socializing, not for worship. I didn't know anything about God at that time, and I wasn't interested.

Then Vera Mae came outside, and I got real interested. She never noticed me, but I saw her. And I liked what I saw. She went and got in a car with a girlfriend and just sat there talking.

I walked over to the car and stood there, just talking to Vera Mae. She seemed glad to see me. But I was more than glad. I knew I had met the girl I wanted to marry.

Just like that.

So I said to her, "Vera Mae, you're going to be my wife someday." Just like that. If Vera Mae was surprised by my sudden proposal, she didn't say so. But she didn't say no either. I guess neither one of us likes to waste time.

Like I said, with our family being gamblers and bootleggers, we weren't known for being church-going people. But that wasn't the real reason why I wasn't religious. And it wasn't because religious people talked so bad about all us Perkinses.

You see, in all my years growing up in Mississippi, I had never heard the simple truth of the gospel: the fact that Jesus Christ could set me free and live His life in me. I grew up knowing nothing about Jesus Christ.

I'd been to religious services as a kid, of course, but I never learned that I could have the power of God in my life, a power that would make a difference in me and in my surroundings. The few times I'd been in church, I had sat and watched everybody else getting emotional. Maybe it's because I always look at things economically, but it was hard for me to see how all that shouting and bench turning I saw in black churches was giving people any kind of incentive to develop. I did not see that life was any better for them than it was for me.

In fact, I had always looked at black Christians as sort of inferior people whose religion had made them gullible and submissive. Religion had made so many of my people humble down to the white-dominated system with all its injustices. Religion had made them cowards and Uncle Toms.

But I was a Perkins and I wasn't like that at all. No way was I like that. So I did not see the black Church as relevant to me and my needs.

And I did not see white Christianity as meaningful either. To me it was part of that whole system that helped dehumanize and destroy black people—that system that identified me as a nigger. So how could the white Church really be concerned about me?

I had lived in the South. I had drunk at separate drinking fountains. I had ridden in the back of buses. And never in the South had I heard one white Christian speak out against the way whites treated blacks as second-class citizens.

I had never accepted that falsehood that I was a second-class citizen. Nor had I ever accepted the myth that I was a nigger. So I did not see the white Church as relevant to me and my needs.

But then something happened after I got back to California.

A Patch of Blue Sky

After meeting Vera Mae and proposing to her, I went back to California. We wrote letters back and forth until we met next in 1951. I was sure happy to see her again. And after having to read all those letters from me, Vera Mae was real glad we could meet face to face once more. She says I don't write worth anything.

We had good times together and began making plans. But then the Korean War came along and changed our plans a bit. I got drafted.

That same year, 1951, when I was through with my basic training, I got a 21-day furlough. Vera Mae and I decided to get married. By the time she got ready, got packed and got out to California on the train, seven days of my furlough were already gone. But we got married anyway and had sort of a whirlwind honeymoon in the few days we had left.

Just two weeks after we were married, Vera Mae returned to her family in Mississippi. I went back to camp and was shipped overseas to Okinawa. And right away, I missed her a whole lot.

Vera Mae was the closest I had ever come to Christianity. In all that time, in my new job and through my whole time in the army, I had no genuine Christian contact—no one who really understood the gospel and the Christian life.

But already my mind was working—and seeking. Yet, because of my background, my motivation was mostly political and economic. So I started to seek for political and social solutions for the world I was in.

While still in the army, I began reading—reading more than some of my buddies who had a lot more formal schooling than I had. I gathered everything I could from the troop information centers and the library.

In my reading, I got my first real description of such things as what communism is, why the United States was in the war, and so on. And my being in military communications gave me my first good chance to exchange ideas with truly informed people holding every sort of personal and political view.

Even so, some of the ideas that stuck with me most at that time I didn't get out of books or bull sessions. I could see first-hand from everyday life how other people viewed money, how they related themselves to the economics of their daily lives.

You see, even in the army I was not a drinking man. Once as a teenager I had finished off a pint of moonshine whiskey and didn't like it. Besides, after watching my aunt's customers year after year, I knew I didn't want to drown my sorrows the way they did.

The practical effects of my lifestyle—no drinking and a very simple scale of living—meant I had extra money. So for the first time in my life, I could turn the tables on the white man. I could loan him money, at interest, all the time remembering the white landowner and the interest he charged us sharecroppers.

Back then, blacks had no choice; that kind of borrowing was necessary to our very life. But here in the army, white men had to borrow money simply because they couldn't handle themselves and their appetites.

I didn't like the army and had no intention of staying. But I made the best of my time, and by the time I was discharged, I could pass for a man with more education than I actually had.

I got out of the army in January 1953 and went straight back to my cousin's house in Monrovia. Vera Mae was still living in Mississippi. I thought at first of going to Mississippi myself and bringing her back with me. Especially since going back would give me a chance to see my father again.

I already knew my father was sick. Jap had had a heart attack and had been staying at Aunt Coot's place ever since. Aunt Coot was sort of our family center and main communicator, so her letters had kept me informed on the family while I was in the army.

But Vera Mae came home to Monrovia soon after I got there, and she brought fresh word of my father. He was getting better, everybody said. So since he seemed out of danger and with Vera Mae back in California, I decided not to go to Mississippi.

Then only a few weeks later, Aunt Coot called to say my father was dead. Jap Perkins had died. I flew back to New Hebron the next day to bury my father. When I got there, I found sort of a mixture of both joy and sadness. They were real glad to see me again after all that time away. But my coming home could not take away their sorrow for another death in the family.

It was a late winter day when I entered Aunt Coot's ramshackle house with its old fireplace. Now, before a country funeral, people come to the home. And every visitor who comes, if he knew the dead person, sits down and listens. Listens to a relative tell the details of how it happened. Over and over again, this will happen with each new visitor.

So Aunt Coot sat me down and began to talk. Only in my case, she started a bit farther back because I had been away so long. I was different now and had moved on to new things. But so much that was still a part of me seemed to settle down in that room as we talked of years and people.

At one point she turned toward me and said, "Jap had hoped you would come home when you got out of the service, Tupy. He'd only been sick for about a week then, and he was getting better, but he was hoping you'd come home. He'd really been wishing for that."

That was a sadness, a sort of wonderment to me. My father *had* wanted me. He really had! Yet I had never known what his true thoughts of me were. I was so uncertain of how he had felt about me, I had just stayed on in California looking for a job.

"Why, Aunt Coot," I asked after a minute, "why didn't you all let me know Daddy wanted me to come home?"

She paused, and I could tell she wasn't quite sure at first how to answer me. "Well," she said finally, "Jap sort of knew Vera Mae was here, and he just thought it natural you'd come to get her. So he didn't make any big special requests.

"When you didn't come and get her, he felt really bad, because he knew then you weren't coming . . ."

What words could say what I felt, sitting there listening to Aunt Coot talking about my father? My daddy. Hurting to see me. And I didn't come home in time.

But I really didn't know he cared. When I was growing up, I always wondered why my daddy didn't want us kids with him. Why he didn't take us back.

Only later I realized it was because of Miss Susan, the woman he married—or was living with. She never had any children of her own. She never really wanted any children. And Daddy was sorta weak, so he could never quite go against her will.

As I look back at it now, I think my father also felt a sense of rejection from his children, because he didn't take care of us as he ought. Now, I had never confronted him with that, so I don't know about it for sure.

My sister Mary and I probably gave Daddy more feeling of being family, more feeling of wanting to keep in touch with him, than some of the others. Yet I did not come home to see him when I got out of the army. So that could have hurt special. And Mary—she got killed in Louisiana. I never did know the details of that.

Daddy's funeral was at Oak Ridge Church, a nice brick church. A cousin of mine preached the funeral. I stood there a long, long time under that February sky, just looking down and thinking how our family had scattered a lot over the years. But they were all together now. My mother. My father. Some uncles. A sister.

And Clyde.

I tried to bury my memories, too, by going back to California as soon as possible and making a good life for Vera Mae and me. It wasn't that we were full of bitterness, because we weren't. California was a place where we could forget all the bitterness— a new land offering a new life, with new memories. We tried to forget all those bad memories from down home.

I threw myself into the thing I considered most important—a good job and good money. I was determined I wouldn't take just any old job, but one that had opportunities to move up.

All my life I had lived with a sort of ceiling above me, a ceiling that said, "You're black, and you can't go no higher." Now I was used to hard work, so I wasn't looking for any easy job. Just one that had a patch of blue sky up above me instead of that ceiling.

A chance to climb.

I started as a janitor with the Shopping Bag Food Store Company. A couple years later I explained to the president of the company that I wanted to stay with them but that I needed to move up. He offered me a job in their welding shop where I learned welding. I showed them I could learn machinery, any machinery, quickly.

Better than that, I drew on my earlier union organizing experience and showed them I could supervise people, too. I started moving up.

By the spring of 1957, I could feel I had pretty good chances in life. And that good feeling was a lot deeper than just the money I was able to earn. I was a provider for my family, I was a man.

And I was going places!

God for a Black Man

I still had lots of questions about life. Questions I couldn't answer. So I wondered a lot. But, for a long time, I didn't recognize those wanderings in the back of my mind as being "religious."

How could I?

My whole family background had been anti-religious. And life, as I grew older, merely reinforced those feelings inside me. In my whole life, apart from Vera Mae, I had never met any religious people who impressed me.

I was convinced that the Church—really the black Church, since that was the only one I knew anything about—was just one more kind of exploitation. I had seen Southern brutality, and the Church had kept silent about it. I was convinced that the problems of my people were political problems. And the black Church I knew, with its emotion and all, never did anything, never said anything about that either.

Obviously, if I had no use for the black Church, I could hardly even imagine something called a "white Christian." It was totally impossible for me to imagine that the white Church, the private club of the oppressors, had anything to do with reality and justice.

Prejudice, of course, knows no boundaries; it can be found anywhere. Experiences of blacks over the years certainly have proved that fact. But at that time in my life, I hadn't developed a total hatred for all whites. You see, in California, I was finally getting somewhere, and getting there with the help of white employers.

Those feelings that I had then—they were mostly directed against the South, against the Southern system. I couldn't see any peaceful way to change the South. So I was convinced that someday there would be a black uprising south of the Mason-Dixon line. And I was anxious for that day to come.

Those were just my thoughts then. I didn't actually involve myself in any action along those lines, because my first priority was my own economic development. Yet I *was* gradually moving toward a notion of black separatism, a total anti-white position that would have included all whites in its hatred. But God stepped in before I got that far. Those years in California gave us a unique time to be developed and prepared by God without the pressure of hatred and malice. It also gave us exposure to a world much bigger than the one we grew up in.

I was with a good company and moving right up. Vera Mae was a trained cosmetologist, fixing hair and planning to have her own shop soon. We had friends, good friends, and a nice house.

We were making it in life. And we were bringing up our kids in a far better state than we had ever known when we were kids ourselves. Our kids and family became the center of our lives, our whole lives.

I suppose the first step in our spiritual development was our involvement with some religious cult groups. The first one we got into was the Jehovah's Witnesses.

Vera Mae got to be good friends with a lady down the street who was very much into it.

We had a class in our house and went to Kingdom Hall—the whole bit. But after a while, other things just sort of faded it out. The Lord was back of it all.

Our youth and energy and enthusiasm led us into a lot of things. I organized a club with a bunch of guys where I worked, and we had dances and stuff like that. At this time I was pretty shy and had a real problem with stuttering. But I always made a lot of friends.

I continued to be interested in politics and sports and kept up on both in the newspapers. In fact, we named our little girl "Joan Inette" after one of my favorite football players, Jon Arnette.

But Vera Mae and I were both still searching for something deeper and greater in life. I did some studies in Christian Science and read a lot about Father Divine. I was trying everything. I know one thing: If I hadn't become a Christian, I would have become a Black Muslim. Their strict devotion and discipline have always appealed to me.

I even became involved in Science of the Mind. And with this, I began to associate religion with success. Success and money and "making it" were my religion, but I was not happy. I had no peace inside.

After our marriage, Vera Mae kept going to church, but only haphazardly. So, though I was looking into some of the cults, I would attend Second Baptist Church, Monrovia, with her and I even did some ushering there. Vera Mae liked the choirs there.

Then in the spring of 1957, God began to show me the unimaginable. And He began it in a quiet way, first through our oldest son, Spencer, and then through a good friend at work, Calvin Bourne.

You see, about this time, Spencer began going to a children's Bible class at a little church just down the street from where we lived. He was real happy about going there, and we didn't mind anything that made Spencer happy.

In those days, we never said a blessing or a verse of Scripture or anything at the table. We just ate. But after he started going to this children's Bible class, Spencer would come home and say verses before we began to eat.

I watched our son. I could see something was developing in him that was beautiful, something I knew nothing about. I'd had no real experience before of seeing Christianity at work like that in a person's life—at work in a way that was beautiful . . . and good.

Spencer kept after me to go with him to his Bible class. And because I loved him so much, I finally decided to go. Besides, his life had become so radiant I wanted to go and find out what they were teaching him down there. I found they were teaching the Bible.

Calvin, meanwhile, had been inviting me for years to go to his church, the Bethlehem Church of Christ Holiness in Pasadena. Vera Mae and the kids had already been going there themselves. Now Calvin finally got me to go with him too.

It was the first time we hit upon some zealous Christians. These were folks who you could feel loved and cared for you. The mothers of the church—Mother Johnson, Mother Bilb, Mother Foster and Mother Holloway—were just like parents to us. They took us under their wing, inviting us over for Sunday dinner and all.

At Bethlehem Church of Christ Holiness, I got to know Rev. Matthew Richardson, the pastor, and Rev. James Howard, his assistant and a teacher in the Sunday School. These black men told me how they had found "new meaning in life through Christ." And their words had a ring to them. I was curious. This was all new to me. But I was always interested in new ideas. So I agreed to join an adult Bible study class, one that was being taught by Rev. Howard on the life of the apostle Paul.

I was now already 27 years old, yet this was my first encounter with the Bible as a real book. Prior to this time, I had looked on the Bible as a superstitious book, full of make-believe and old wives' tales. Why would any intelligent person bother to read it? Only religious people did that. And, like I said, I had always thought of them as being inferior people, people who could not make it in society.

Most of the people I knew in the company where I worked were just so-so religious. They were not people who carried Bibles in their hands or gave out tracts. And yet they were the successful people in the company.

But once I make up my mind to do anything, I do it good. And I was a good student. I studied my Bible through April, May and right on into summertime. It was the first time I ever searched the Scriptures for myself. And I enjoyed it.

Every day I studied my Bible, carefully working my way through the New Testament. And every week I met with the study group, joined in the discussions and asked questions, mostly questions about Paul.

The thing that really hit me about Paul was this motivation he had. By this time in life, I was pretty super-motivated myself, but I was motivated for my own economic betterment. As I read and studied the life of Paul, I saw that he was super-motivated, too. But his motivation was unselfish. And it was a religious motivation.

A religious motivation! That really got to me. How could religion mean so much to anyone, even Paul? The question hounded me all summer long.

Paul had drive. And he had even more enthusiasm. But what was it that made him tick? I had to find out.

To help me in my studies on Paul, Vera Mae went down to this bookstore in Monrovia and bought me a commentary on the book of Acts from Mary Feastal, who ran the store. Mary was later to become a very good friend. Even back then, the Lord was already at work weaving our lives together with others for His own purpose.

Meanwhile, summer moved into fall. More study, more work, more questions, more discussions. This guy Paul was getting to me.

Paul endured so much just for religion. Why? I still didn't see anything in religion that would cause a man to want to give up his life and endure all that Paul suffered. As I looked at religion, it was not something to suffer for; it was something to suffer with.

One night as I was home lying on my son's bed in the back room, the Spirit of God for the first time took the Word of God and really spoke to me. I was reading from Galatians 2:20 where Paul says, "I am crucified with Christ: nevertheless I live; yet not I, but Christ liveth in me: and the life which I now live in the flesh I live by the faith of the Son of God, who loved me, and gave himself for me."

You know, I'd never heard that before. I'd never heard about an in-living Christ. I'd never heard that being a Christian was Christ living in me, and me living out my life in Christ.

Well, I realized I didn't have that life. All I had was an ulcer—and I wasn't 30 yet.

The kind of life Paul was talking about came from total yielding to Christ—from just the opposite of my self-pushing. In spite of my motivation, my hope, I didn't have Paul's contentment. I had to seek harder. I had studied hard, and because I now knew more about the Bible than some of the Christians in our church, they apparently thought I was a Christian, too. But I knew I wasn't. Paul had already told me that.

That Sunday I went back to our mission Sunday School. Vera Mae was home, pregnant with Derek, so I went to church alone that day. The pastor preached a sermon that morning on Romans 6:23: "For the wages of sin is death; but the gift of God is eternal life through Jesus Christ our Lord."

That verse of Scripture spoke to my whole experience. It hit me hard right in my interest and motivation, and the Holy Spirit began to speak to my heart.

Wages. Pay. Who gets what for what, and who decides how much. Yes, I knew about wages. Wages were a dime and a buffalo nickel. Wages were what I got as a young boy, when I was old enough to work hard, but still young enough that a white employer might still excuse himself from paying his black laborer a decent wage.

And the white man who paid that wage made sure his black hired help ate their meal far enough away, so they wouldn't disturb his white house in his white world—a world in which there was no good life and no big house for any black man no matter how hard he worked. In that world, the white man called the shots and set the wages and lived the way he did because he had the capital to be in charge—*not* because he was a harder worker than a black man.

Yes, I sure did know about wages. But—wages of *sin*? What was this preacher talking about?

I thought I knew about the "wages of sin." Union organizers had talked to me at the foundry about stopping exploitation. But all my boyhood experiences had taught me better than those other factory workers what that word meant. Exploitation was sin.

But was there other sin? *My* sin? Back and forth from life to Scripture my mind went that morning. And all those months of study on the life of Paul fed into my thinking, too.

For the first time I understood that my sin was not necessarily and altogether against myself or against my neighbor. My sin was against a holy God who loved me, who had already paid for my sins. I was sinning in the face of His love.

I didn't want to sin anymore. I wanted to give my life to Christ, so He could take care of my sin. I sensed the beginning of a whole new life, a new structure of life, a life that could fill that emptiness I had even on payday.

God for a black man? Yes, God for a black man! *This* black man! Me!

That morning I said yes to Jesus Christ.

Winners and Losers

I had peace. I didn't have any solutions yet to what I'd been struggling with in my life, but I had an inward peace for the first time.

After church, I went home and told Vera Mae what had happened to me. Calvin Bourne came over, too, all happy and excited. "The brother got saved this morning!" he said.

At first, Vera Mae didn't seem too impressed, almost as though what we were saying to her just went in one ear and out the other. It didn't faze her one bit.

Later she explained what was going through her heart and mind just then: "I wasn't thinking anything about the brother getting saved. I was a Christian from a long time back, but I didn't have enough sense not to yoke myself with an unbeliever or even to pray that the Lord would save him. That shows you how far away I was myself!"

But it was true: I was genuinely saved that Sunday morning. And it caused me and the whole family to really dedicate our lives to the Lord.

I moved into my new life like I did everything else—as hard as I could. I began sharing Christ with people in the area where I lived. And those church members who had thought I was already a Christian could now see some *real* changes in me.

Now, I had already been turned off to liquor during my bootlegging boyhood, so drinking had never been a problem for me. But I did enjoy the excitement of gambling and horse racing. Even though I had it under control enough so it didn't wreck our family budget, there was a good boost in our economic position when I dropped gambling entirely.

I didn't drop gambling because anybody preached against it. That kind of push never really works over the long haul. True Christian change works more like an old oak tree in the spring, when the new life inside pushes off the old dead leaves that still hang on.

That's how God worked with me. I simply had better things to do now. For one thing, I began reading everything I could get my hands on. I had so much to learn. I kept going back to the bookstore where Vera Mae had bought the commentary for me. Mary Feastal did more than sell books to me. She prayed for me, and she worked on my speech. She helped me with my pronunciation and taught me how to practice speaking without stuttering. My speech really began to improve.

Vera Mae and I also became involved in the Child Evangelism Fellowship, sharing Jesus with little children. This was soon after that Sunday in November 1957 when I met Christ. Vera Mae's friend Wilnora Price, who lived on our street, had been attending Child Evangelism classes and liked them. She invited us to attend, too.

Vera Mae had been saved through Child Evangelism as a young girl and had always loved their use of flannel-boards. But Child Evangelism was new to me. Yet when I looked at it, I saw what I had seen in the adult class that had helped to bring me to God: an emphasis on learning, on getting something solid. This was way different from the emotionalism of the black Church I had rejected years before.

Vera Mae and I both began teaching classes among the black children of Monrovia, one each afternoon at 5:00—and going to the leadership training workshops every Tuesday night. That is one thing about us: When we get involved, it is all or nothing.

In those workshops I found something I never expected besides the Bible learning. I met white Christians. It's hard to describe how odd, how different that whole experience was for me. Not just white church members, but white *Christians*—people who said that God had actually changed their lives.

Every Tuesday night I sat with my white teacher, Mr. Wayne Leitch. God was taking me step by step. First He showed me black people changed by the gospel. Now He was showing me that it had power even for whites.

Mr. Leitch didn't hold me back with any rigid ideas of what he thought my abilities ought to be. When he saw what I could handle, he offered to work with me during afternoons as well. My job by this time was in El Monte, where he lived; so I would stop by his school at 3:30 every day after work to learn, think and talk man to man, Christian to Christian. We met together like this for the next two years.

Along with working, studying and teaching, I also began to do lay preaching at Sunday night services, sharing my testimony at white and black churches. I didn't do real good at the beginning.

One of my first opportunities came when I was asked to preach the sermon at our church on New Year's Eve, 1958. Just before I was to start, Calvin Bourne discovered that he'd forgotten the wine for our communion service. So he dashed out across the street to get some.

After he left, I got up to preach on "A Voice Crying in the Wilderness." I just went through my outline. I guess it only took me about 30 seconds. That seemed kinda short, so I went through it again. Then a third time. And having nothing more to say, I sat down.

About that time, Calvin came puffing back and thought he hadn't missed a thing. Well, he hadn't missed much. The rest of the service went on for a while, and finally he leaned over and whispered to me, "Hey, Brother, aren't you gonna preach tonight?"

"I did already," I said.

Calvin's still wondering about that one.

From the spring of 1958 until 1960, Monrovia—especially the black community—got to know me. For a while I had Child Evangelism classes nearly every afternoon in the week. I seemed to be more effective with boys—boys heavily dominated my classes. But response was not what pushed me on. Response or no response, the main joy for me was to be able to tell the salvation story.

Other black Christians helped me to see the needs for person-to-person adult evangelism. With four of them—Rev. Curry Brown, Rev. George Moore, Mrs. Elizabeth Wilson and Mr. Jim Winston—I helped form an informal group that we later called the "Fisherman's Gospel Crusade." We knew that blacks around Monrovia needed to be confronted with the real Christ, the Christ for them. There were churches, of course, but there was still a great need for the whole gospel to be communicated person to person. So we began a simple program of Sunday afternoon evangelism.

Each Sunday we met on Mrs. Wilson's porch. Then we'd decide, if we didn't already have an invitation, which family we would visit that afternoon to share our faith. In this ministry we learned to depend on each other. It was a group effort. In the home, one or two would share a personal testimony. They generally let me make some comments on Scripture portions. And we all joined in the conversation.

Many blacks in the area, if they had any contact with churches, were used to just listening to sermons. Non-religious types just ignored religion, the same as I had done. But we gave all of them a chance to actually have some give-and-take with the Bible in terms of their own lives, asking their own questions, finding answers for themselves.

We weren't trying to form a new church group. We were only trying to turn our own faith loose right where we lived. People who did find new life in Christ in this house evangelism would join local churches, so churches themselves often gave us the names of friends or relatives to visit. Other times, we might get an invitation directly from a wife or husband to come and talk with their family or to a roomful of people.

All this kept me busy, but I still looked for other opportunities. One of these was destined to change the shape of my whole life. It began when a bookstore owner put me in touch with the Christian Businessmen's Committee of Arcadia-Monrovia. There I met John McGill who later became one of my best friends and was on the board of Child Evangelism Fellowship. There I had a chance for real Christian fellowship with a group that was at the time an all-white group. For a while I was the only black member.

I really got involved with these Christian businessmen. Soon they were also asking me to share my testimony here and there. I was also teaching Bible classes every night. After a while I found myself constantly on the go. You know, every Sunday night, every Sunday morning, through the week, some place, some church, some group. I got so busy I didn't have time anymore to look at the system around me. I almost forgot my upbringing.

Then two of the Christian businessmen I knew, Ed Anthony and Dean Saum, asked me to go with them to visit California prison camps in the San Bernardino Mountains. The boys in these camps are only 13 to 17 years old. They help take care of those firebreaks cutting across the mountains.

I soon found out why my friends asked me to go with them in these camps. A majority of the prison population was black. A black witness to Christ was needed. And that witness was me.

We held Sunday morning Bible classes in a Quonset hut for the young men of the camps. Each time we went, I shared a brief testimony and spoke from the Scriptures. The young prisoners were often suspicious of me. And some of them came to the meetings simply because they were bored and had nothing else to do. But I began to see young men's lives change.

One of the first times I spoke, there were 30 or 40 young men listening. I poured all my effort into that sermon. When I was finished, two of them came down to ask Christ to change their lives.

They were crying. But it wasn't the response, it wasn't the emotion that had the real effect on me. It was the story of their own lives that started me wondering about my real values and goals as a Christian.

These young fellows were on their way to being real losers in society. And in their minds, I was what I looked—somebody who had made it. To them, this businessman-preacher was just another visitor from that other world, the world of Winners. And they were Losers.

They didn't know my background, but I knew what I was and what I had been. So, from that point on, I began to ask myself more and more what special responsibility God had for me. These boys in prison camp often had backgrounds just like mine. Their voices and their accents sounded like guys I grew up with. Some of them had come right from the same deep South I had known, or were the sons of blacks who had fled that closed society. Like me, they came without many skills, without much education. Like me, they didn't have a strong religious background.

And, like me, they had dreams of "making it" in California. But a funny thing happened on their way to Success. It's called Failure.

Now, I couldn't analyze all the reasons I ended up different. Maybe my family background gave me some extra drive and ambition. But, you see, I couldn't claim credit for that. It was something handed down to me just as money is inherited. And on top of that, God had now made me one of His own. I couldn't really feel that I had survived because of any personal goodness on my part.

But I had more than survived. God had let me succeed where these young men had failed. I had a good job, good opportunities. My wife had a good job and all that, too. And here these young men were—in jail, in trouble. Yet God loved these young men no less than He loved me.

So if God had done all this for me, and if He loved these others no less than He did me, what did all this mean? What did it say to *my* plans for *my* "good" Christian life?

Well, first thing, I saw more clearly that the roots of many of the black man's problems in the ghetto were really the unsolved problems of the South I had left. I couldn't escape a conviction growing up inside of me that God wanted me back in Mississippi, to identify with my people there, and to help them break the cycle of despair—not by encouraging them to leave, but by showing them new life right where they were.

Real soon the conviction became a command. I remember the night it happened—the night God spoke to me through His Word about going back to Mississippi and starting a ministry for Him there. I was giving my testimony that night to an all-white church in Arcadia, California.

Standing before the crowd of people gathered there, I used as my text Romans 10:1-2, where Paul says, "Brethren, my heart's desire and prayer to God for Israel is, that they might be saved. For I bear them record that they have a zeal for God, but not according to knowledge."

God took the power of Paul's love for His people and shot it through me, saying, "John, my desire for you is that you go back to Mississippi, because I bear your people witness that they have a zeal for God, but it is not enlightened."

I was reminded of the emotionalism of many of the congregations I had seen and heard. I recalled the fact that most black preachers pastured four or five churches at the same time and yet had little or no opportunity for real Bible training.

God was speaking to me. Calling me.

I was never again satisfied in California.

A Hard Command

I began sharing my new vision of a Mississippi ministry with some friends and soon found out that many of them had a lot of reasons why I should forget the whole matter. After all, I had a wife and a growing family. I was a Christian witness right where I was—and that was certainly enough of doing God's work.

My good friends in the Fisherman's Gospel Crusade were sad. By this time we had become a good team. But they would not want to stand in God's way, so they pledged some monthly support as well as their prayers.

Among a few white Christians in California during that time there seemed to be a growing awareness of the need to share the gospel with the black community. I spoke to two white churches—Calvary Bible Church in Burbank, pastored by Dr. Jack MacArthur, and Arcadia Union Church, pastored by Rev. Glen Zachary. Between them they promised $75 a month, which was a main part of our support.

I knew that Vera Mae had been so happy when I accepted Christ. But she hadn't really counted on it leading us back to Mississippi. Many of her own relatives over the years who had moved north and west from Mississippi had struggled for years to gain things like respectability and owning their own home.

Vera Mae wanted very much to show to them that marrying a Perkins from that family of gamblers and bootleggers could turn out okay after all. And now we were just beginning to make it—a real sign that Vera Mae *had* made a good choice after all. We had continued living simply on our rising income, so we had been able to move from our little house in Pomona into a big, twelve-room, two-and-a-half bathroom house on Los Angeles Street. It was mortgaged, but it was ours. And we had already planned how we were going to fix it up.

So I knew at the time Vera Mae was not wildly enthusiastic about the prospects of our returning to Mississippi. But I really didn't know all of the feelings she had then, the pain and conflict in her heart. I never knew how bad she was hurting until a lot later.

Going back to Mississippi was a must for me. God was calling me back. But it was "my" call. Never "our" call.

I felt the call. Vera Mae didn't. And the more I talked about going back, the more she rebelled against it.

To make matters worse, I got real sick. I began losing weight, a lot of weight. And I became so weak, I could hardly stand up.

Vera Mae carried me to the Long Beach Veterans' Hospital many times. The first diagnosis was ulcers. But then the ulcers healed.

I continued to lose weight until I had lost more than 40 pounds. The doctors checked my heart and other vital organs. Everything was okay; yet I was wasting away.

I talked of quitting my job. But Vera Mae would say, "No, Toop [her version of Tupy], you can't quit your job. We've got all these younguns to feed."

We were expecting our fifth child—Debbie—by then. So even though I was sick, I kept going to work. Besides, I liked my job in design and production of shopping baskets for the food company.

But I got weaker and weaker. Finally a day came in November 1959 when I was too weak to stand up. I couldn't get out of bed.

I didn't know then that the Lord had been speaking to Vera Mae. But He was, and the message was clear. She had to let me go, or she might not have me at all.

Later she explained, "The Lord showed me that day that unless I would give in to His calling, to what He was calling Toop—and us—to do, I would have no husband. Either I yielded, or He would take Toop away from me. The thought of losing Toop was bad enough. But the thought of having to raise five children alone was even worse. It was a frightening thought."

I was in bed but awake that morning when Vera Mae came into the bedroom and knelt by our bed. "Toop," she said, "I'm going to pray for you."

And then she prayed aloud, so God and I could both hear: "Lord, it's a hard struggle for me to say yes, but I'm going to say yes. I'm willing to go. I don't want to go, but I'm willing. Lord, I'm saying yes to you."

Then she prayed some more, asking the Lord to raise me up again and use me any way He willed. When she finished praying, her burden was gone. The great choking feeling in her heart was gone. That prayer of surrender, after what had started out as a hard command from God, ended up giving her real peace with God like she hadn't had since I first told her about my dream.

Vera Mae had found peace. And I was feeling better already. I felt God raising up my body as well as my spirit.

The next day, a few days before Thanksgiving, I was up and walking around. I felt well enough to tell Vera Mae, "I'm going to Mississippi and check things out." Then I got ready to go.

The day I left to go south, Vera Mae—along with Spencer, Joanie, Phillip and Derek—took me down to the little bus station in Monrovia. As we waited for the bus to pull out, I put my arms around the children and Vera Mae—now seven months' pregnant with Debbie—holding my family close and trying to comfort them with my love for them.

I had to make that trip. And we all knew it. But perhaps, as we stood there in that bus depot, holding tight to each other, we sensed this little trial separation was just the beginning, just a taste of some of the bigger trials we would face in the future.

Yes, it was hard for my family to put me on that bus. And, in a way, it was hard for me to go and leave them. We all knew we'd be lonely. Yet for the sake of yielding to God's will, we could not do otherwise.

Yielding to God's will can be hard. And sometimes, it really hurts. But it always brings peace.

By Thanksgiving I was already in Mississippi. My plan was—well, I couldn't explain my plan very well. I didn't have a detailed strategy at first, except to pave the way for moving the family back with me. I spoke in a few churches around my old home-town of New Hebron, talked with people and tried to feel out the best place and the most effective way for me to work.

I was still driven by the image of those broken black lives in the California youth detention camps. And I knew our greatest potential for reaching those young lives—while they were still reachable—lay in Child Evangelism. That need and that means of fulfilling the need convinced me there was a ministry for us among the youth of Mississippi.

Altogether, I stayed six weeks in Mississippi, scouting the territory. Then, on Christmas Eve, I called Vera Mae. "Honey, it's me! Tupy! Can you come on down and pick me up?"

"Sure, Toop, where are you?"

"I'm right here in Monrovia. At the bus station. I just got back."

I heard happiness in her voice, and I knew she was glad to have me safe home again with her and the kids. Thanksgiving had been lonely, but Christmas would be different.

Things started happening fast after I got back. Our fifth child, Deborah, was born the next month—January 26, 1960. I left my job in good standing with the company, and our family prepared to move back to Mississippi. During this time, God met all our needs, and friends encouraged us with their prayers.

By June we had rented out our house. This freed us to go and left us with a little money in the bank. So, on June 6, we loaded up a U-Haul trailer and hitched it to our '56 Chevy. Then Dave Peacock brought an offering by that the Christian businessmen had collected. Just before we left, John McGill slipped $20 into my shirt pocket. We started off, heading due south.

By June 9, we were back in Mississippi—the same Mississippi I had once left "for good."

Under the Skin

Back in Mississippi, Vera Mae and I and the five children went to live with her grandmother down near New Hebron. This was the same old world I had left. The same area where Clyde had been killed. The same area I had once walked out of—for good. Now I was back, not because Mississippi had changed, but because God had changed me and called me back.

Vera Mae hadn't felt called to Mississippi herself, at first, but she had agreed to go back with me anyway. And almost from the word go, *my* ministry became *our* ministry, a *family* ministry. God had called us back to Mississippi as a family!

During the rest of that 1960 summer, Vera Mae and I organized some vacation Bible schools. The short Bible schools were something new to these people. There were churches for black folks all around, but the religion they got there was not for learning; it was just for getting emotional and for socializing. I wanted to catch their hearts with the truth that had caught my heart—that the Bible was for learning, real learning about God.

The children didn't know me personally, but I knew their world, their language, and I had their black skin. In one place near Brookhaven, at McCall Creek, our vacation Bible school started with 10 children the first day. At the end of two weeks we had more than 120, including a number of adults. That fall there were more opportunities for witness in the black schools.

Now, you can't really understand my experiences or the experiences of my children and other black children in Mississippi unless you know a little bit of the history of education in the state. There have been many changes, especially since the late 1950s when Mississippi was forced to revamp its school system. Many of these changes have been for the better; but to see the whole picture you have to realize that most of the changes were made reluctantly, under the growing threat of federal pressure. And change by force hasn't always changed the attitudes of white society.

But before these changes, it was a fact that if schools for black children had had to depend on pubic tax funds alone, they just would never have existed. Many black schools in Mississippi were a tribute to private effort more than public support. After Emancipation, and at other times, missions and similar organizations provided people and money for our black education. Tougaloo College, Mary Holmes College and other schools were started and funded by benevolent white Christians from the north. Christians and private organizations provided tuition aid, teacher training, teachers' salaries, books and school buildings. And the local black communities provided other help, like labor to raise buildings and maintain them.

For instance, one really big foundation was a fund of several million dollars set up by Julius Rosenwald, chairman of Sears-Roebuck and Company. He did not donate school buildings outright, but had conditions attached to his grants that would stimulate local efforts. In the black community, "local effort" almost always meant the churches, because they were the only, or strongest, social organizations. So the growth of black schools in Mississippi before the late '50s was often tied in with churches. Schools were sometimes built alongside the church; church and school were overlapping parts of the same community in those places.

On May 17, 1954, in *Brown vs. Board of Education of Topeka,* the U.S. Supreme Court ruled that "separate but equal" schools were *not* equal and were, thereby, unconstitutional. Now you can't really add up in dollars and cents all the injustices of the old "separate but equal" educational system, but some money amounts can give you at least a hint. In the year before that famous court decision, official Mississippi Department of Education figures show that the state had 544,405 students registered in public schools, divided almost evenly between black and white children. But though equal numbers of children were involved, there was an unequal distribution of money spent on their education:

TRANSPORTATION
White: $4,476,753
Black: $1,179,826

INSTRUCTION
White: $23,536,022
Black: $8,816,670

SALARY AVERAGE
White: $2,109
Black: $1,553

These wildly different expenditures were all done according to "proper" procedure. State educational funds were granted on the basis of the number of total students in a county. But then, separate budgets were made up, using different minimum standards for black and white schools. Since each black student "required" less money for his education than a white student "required," it turned out that those counties with the highest percentage of black students actually had the best schools for whites; more money had been "donated" by the larger number of black students and it was shared among a smaller group of white students.

The state did try to smooth out some of the inequities—that is, the inequities between white schools. See, those counties with a higher proportion of whites had less money per pupil for white education, and they resented that. So "equalization" funds were set up to even out the differences between white schools in different counties. You don't have to be a radical at all—just a human being—to understand why people of my generation and even younger felt discouraged or bitter when even that beautiful word "equality" was abused, in our eyes, simply to mean equality among whites.

Of course, a root problem is that Mississippi has always been one of the poorer states in per capita income. So it naturally has had less money overall for everything, including education. With that kind of cash scarcity, there never seemed to be enough money to provide a good education for everybody who wanted one.

Many Mississippi whites, especially middle class and lower, resented any suggestion that they were "exploiters." They sometimes felt that even they and their children were not getting an adequate amount; that they were only working and striving for their minimum, their bottom-level necessity. But any way you look at it, even those whites who only got an "average" education, a "minimum" education of eighth grade, got it at the expense of blacks. That education helped them to get the right jobs and make their way in the world.

With this system so firmly entrenched in the thinking of white Mississippi, you can understand a little how reaction to that 1954 Supreme Court decision could be so strong, even hysterical. Governor Hugh White stood up tall and reassured everyone that Mississippi was "never going to have integration in its schools." For quite a while it was possible that the state would close down the entire public school system simply to avoid integrating it.

The chief legal officer of the state, Attorney General James Plemon Coleman, joined in the general outcry to resist, though his statements were mild compared with some of the real extremists. He said that the court decision was "unconstitutional" and urged Mississippi to defy it, though adding that it should be defied "by every legal and constitutional means available." I'm not sure what kinds of constitutional means of "defiance" are still open after a Supreme Court ruling like that, but that's what the man said.

This same Coleman later became governor, then a federal judge. While on that federal bench, he played a crucial part in my life as part of a two-to-one majority denying my appeal to federal courts when I couldn't get justice in the state courts.

Anyway, the schools didn't close down. They worked out some bureaucratic compromises that "unified" the previous separate school districts. Segregation continued, of course, by assigning pupils to various schools in the new districts that were integrated only in an administrative way.

The state did hope for sympathy in their cause by beginning a sharp increase in expenditures for black schools. School buildings went up everywhere—brick buildings in every county, it seemed. And every county got school buses. There were some real visible changes all over the state from those old one- or two-room "cotton house" schools to full-scale buildings. And that alone meant there was a frantic need for more black teachers. Every black youngster who dreamed of college waited to be a teacher.

So when I got back to Mississippi in 1960, there was a lot of movement and change. There was so much to be done and so much to fear in the poverty, illiteracy and rigid segregationist feelings that still were around. But the new schools and the new focus of interest on education helped give me a boost in my first project—child evangelism.

That first fall, when I went with my children to register them for school, I sat and listened to the orientation session. It was held in the church next door to the school, it being one of the older schools I told you about. The principal there seemed to be under special pressure to prove himself acceptable to the community, so he was real careful to try to show himself as a good community man. This was just the opportunity I needed—this man could not very well turn down my offer to enrich the school program.

So after the orientation session I introduced myself to the principal. "How about some Bible classes for the students in your school?"

"Fine."

I smiled inside and began preparing right away to teach Bible classes in the school at New Hymn, near Pinola. We did well there, and our newfound reputation helped open doors in other schools. Soon we had classes going in the counties of Copiah, Rankin, Scott, Covington, Simpson and Jeff Davis.

I also became involved at Prentiss Institute, a black junior college. The founders, Mr. and Mrs. J. E. Johnson, had been students of George Washington Carver and Booker T. Washington. Mr. Johnson had died, but Mrs. Johnson was still active at Prentiss. For years she had felt a need for a kind of spiritual emphasis at the college, though she wasn't sure what kind of emphasis or how to search for it.

Mrs. Johnson invited me to speak at a Religious Emphasis Week at Prentiss, and it seemed to show a real spirit of revival, with something like 40 kids accepting Christ. On the final Sunday night, these kids gave their testimony to the whole group at the meeting. After that, I became the regular chaplain of Prentiss while continuing my other work.

With the Bible classes at Prentiss, as with all my work, I moved on the assumption that Christianity is a fellowship of believers, not just a collection of individuals. My work as a Bible teacher and pastor didn't just lean on whatever skills I had in class teaching; just as important was letting people know I was also involved with the needs of their daily lives. Our income, our lifestyle, our needs and problems matched a lot of these people's concerns; we could live among them more like friends helping friends than like well-off outsiders coming to do good.

Then in February 1961, we found a house in Mendenhall, the county seat of Simpson County. Now we were able to move out of the house we had been crowded in with Vera Mae's grandmother. Most of Mendenhall spreads over a long slope, with the main business street stretching down from the courthouse at the top. Further down, across the railroad tracks, across the highway and along some narrow and winding streets, is the black section of town.

That whole area brought back memories for Vera Mae. Our house was just down the street from a two-story cinderblock building that used to be a dormitory for black high school students—and Vera Mae had been one of them years before. And for three years, until she finished high school, Vera Mae was one of the students in that dorm, going home weekends.

We lived in a small house in Mendenhall, and we rented another place for more space. It was a small storefront just down the street, and that gave me some office space and storage for supplies, as well as space for Bible club meetings.

And in the next year, more expansion. We bought a large tent that we could set up for meetings, but not your usual "tent meetings" with flashy singers and a big production and all. No way. We had preaching all right, but the whole idea was more for teaching and Bible classes than for a big show.

And people would come. The tent would be in each place for at least two weeks. None of this flying around that some groups do. We got to know the people, and we kept up the tent ministry for a couple of years.

But in that same year, 1962, something big began, in a very small way. I knew we would have to get our own property sometime and stop renting. So I took the money I had in my savings account and, for less than $900, I was able to buy five small lots on the outer edge of the black section of Mendenhall. There was no paved street—trucks with supplies, if they came in wet weather, had to unload up the street.

We contracted for a builder to put up the shell of a large house. Then, with some of the teenage boys I had been working with, we finished up the interior ourselves. These young men— such as Ernest Jones, Leonard Stapleton, Artis Fletcher, Herbert Jones, Dolphus and Melvin Weary—were more to me than just guys who came to Bible classes.

You see, I knew that if the Bible I was teaching could ever really do something here, it would have to be a visible truth. I knew that if I only had students, even lots of students, the whole thing could drift away like many other "religious" programs. I knew that I had to develop fellow workers, not just Bible club students.

Before we even finished the interior, I moved our family into the house and began applying the rent from the two previous places to the mortgage on the house. That house was big enough to hold the weekly youth meetings in the downstairs living room. I knew that God had already blessed our ministry in the lives of young people, but it was still a nice feeling to have this new building as a physical sign of our hope for Mendenhall.

It's Nice to Have Friends

With the growth of our work, money again became crucial. Late in 1963 I knew I would have to go back to some of my contacts in California for more support for our next big need: a school building. Vera Mae and the older students could continue the Bible classes.

So once again I headed for California. And a better life was my goal, just as before. Only this time the better life in my vision was back in Mississippi. My goal was $3,000 for bricks and other material for the Bible institute building; milder weather in Mississippi made construction costs a bit less than elsewhere.

I had a lot of experience working with people, from my days as a union steward on down, but fund-raising was different. In my prayers I was conscious of the human barriers I faced, and the need to trust God if this whole project was to succeed. God would have to multiply the few contacts I had. I had no fancy brochures, no movies or slides of our work. I could only open myself up to those who would listen, and tell them of the needs in Mississippi.

A prime stop was the Calvary Bible Church of Burbank, California, pastored by Dr. Jack MacArthur. This church was interested in rural ministries, and I became one of their rural ministry representatives—and continued as such for the next seven years. The church also sponsored a radio broadcast called the "Voice of Calvary," so it seemed natural, under their sponsorship, to call our own ministry the "Voice of Calvary" as soon as the next building went up.

And the pledges came in. With that money, along with some of my own I had left over after selling our house in California, I returned with $6,000, not just the $3,000 I had aimed for. With the difference, we could buy a secondhand bus. That very winter, early in the new year of 1964, we began working on the brick building alongside our frame house.

Around this time we found ourselves organizing a church, though that hadn't been part of our original plan. Much of what we wanted to do didn't fit in to the traditional church patterns, and we found that many people in the community were already viewing our work as a church, with the Bible classes and all; so, in 1964, we formed a new congregation, the Berean Bible Church.

While the church was growing, I was invited to speak in Dallas at a school where one of my young student co-workers, Artis Fletcher, had gone. There in Dallas, a businessman, Mr. Kirk Lamb, heard our story and gave us enough money for yet another building that we could use for a chapel. We also bought some more land with that money, land on which we could build a gymnasium later.

We named our new school building the "Glenna Bell Hall" after Mrs. Glenna Bell Leitch, the wife of my Bible teacher. I worked with two white men to organize some long-range Bible classes. Rev. Kenneth Noyes, a mission worker, and Rev. James Spencer, a Presbyterian minister, became my first white co-workers. But that effort didn't last long.

In the 1960s the Ku Klux Klan, and people who claimed to speak for them, were far from dead. In fact, the civil rights movement had brought with it, you might say, a rise in the old racist organizations. Rev. Spencer was no outsider. He had roots in the local area, which meant that he was more vulnerable to threats against his family and his career. Phone calls in the night would wake him. I could see he was feeling the strain. Finally it was too much. He was driven to leave us.

Later we were able to add other courses to our Bible classes, when a highly respected black teacher, Mrs. Annie Bell Harper, began teaching English and speech for us. A local black school that she and her husband had founded was named in their honor, and it kept the name of Harper School until court-ordered integration in the '70s brought in some white students and it became a junior high school. Naturally, the all-white school board and the white parents could not tolerate their children attending a school whose name honored a black person, so the name was changed to Mendenhall Junior High School.

I knew that the heart of our work would be the growing community of young people and faithful older Christians right in Mendenhall. But I kept up the school ministry that I had first begun the summer I got back. Vera Mae and other co-workers helped me.

These youngsters were starved for real Christian guidance, and I encouraged them to write to me after each program we gave. Besides our talks, flannel-graph stories and songs, we offered free New Testaments to anyone who asked, but they would have to write to me for them. We could usually find church and mission groups willing to give us Bibles for this ministry. Finding financial support to attack hunger and economic ills wasn't so easy. But we could always get Bibles.

Here and there, I did catch glimpses of white Christians trying to get a fresh look, a look through the eyes of God, at the time-honored ideas they had accepted from their upbringing.

There was one local white minister in particular, Dr. Robert Odenwald. He was pastor of the First Baptist Church of Mendenhall. At first, he was kinda cold toward me and the work of Voice of Calvary. Not hostile really—like so many were. Just cold.

Since I had some business matters to talk over with Dr. Odenwald about one of our community projects, I made up my mind to really try to get to know him. Perhaps there was a possibility of establishing some common ground between us.

So one day after prayer, I went uptown to see Dr. Odenwald. I walked into his outer office and asked his secretary if I could see him. I had already noticed when I first walked in that the black janitor had seen me, and I knew he must have felt funny, because black men—even black ministers of the gospel—didn't go visiting white ministers of the gospel.

But I went on in to Dr. Odenwald's office, knowing that he had shown some interest, at least, in our work. I told him what I was doing and why I believed God had called me to my work. I explained that we had a Christian ministry in Mendenhall trying to reach young people for Christ. And I told him about some of the areas we went into and the people we met—areas and people who were just part of a different world to him.

I didn't ask Dr. Odenwald for support. I hadn't come for that. Our conversation began to drift more to theology, to our faith. I realized that he was interested in whether or not I was a real, Bible-preaching Christian—he really didn't know how to label me. I told him that I, too, shared his faith in Christ alone, that Ephesians 2:8 and 9—saved by grace alone—was my message, too.

It was a long conversation. We went on and on, finding more and more in each other of what was down under, under each other's skin. As we talked, he became radiant—like it was a fire inside him to know we were preaching the same gospel.

He showed me a book he was reading, the true story of a black preacher named John Jasper. Jasper was one of those black preachers working right at the time of Emancipation, one of the most famous black preachers of that time—even whites came to hear him preach. For years he could only preach on his days off from the tobacco factory, but he finally ended up with his very own church.

Jasper's boss, on hearing of Jasper's conversion and preaching, didn't discourage him, but told him, "Preach the Word, John, preach the Word." And that white minister turned to me there in his study and said to me—"Preach the Word, John, preach the Word."

All this Dr. Odenwald shared with me. Then the two of us prayed together—there. As I left, the man was crying. I had never seen a white man so moved. And me—I thanked God for showing me Himself at work.

Dr. Odenwald and I had more conversations after that over the next few months. I wasn't bothered when I learned that whites were beginning to notice our friendship. God was at work.

It was a real struggle though for this man, all wrapped up as he was in his traditions. But he did try to express something of God's love for *all* people in a couple of sermons. He even voiced the contradiction he had seen between his own biblical convictions and the social attitudes he and his congregation accepted unthinkingly from the surrounding white society.

It wasn't what some might call big, bold, radical, but it was obvious enough. Cautiously, but surely, he had tried to take the major step of trying to preach the real meaning of Christian love as it applied to the sin of racism.

Only he met with absolute resistance. In fact, some whites didn't see any connection at all between their minister's new sermons and the Bible. All they saw was that the pastor was acting "strange."

I could tell this man was under great emotional stress, really strained. But I never understood at the time what all he was going through. Then one night as I was driving along in my car from a Bible class at Premiss Institute with the radio on, I heard the news. Dr. Odenwald had committed suicide! I wept in my heart for this man who had tried so hard to build a bridge of understanding between his people and ours, the same kind of bridge we had built so slowly and so carefully between the two of us. Here was a man who, I thought, might have helped link our two communities together.

"Why, God?" I asked. "Why?" I didn't know why.

I went to Dr. Odenwald's wake. The casket was closed, and it seemed closed, too, against any answers I might find there. I was the only black there, but that was all right—white funerals are a little different from other white events. I guess it goes back to plantation days. In those days, when the white plantation owner died, they'd ask all the black folks to come because it would be so nice to say that the man was loved by black and white alike.

It's too bad, death is the only time some people think of that. Love, I mean.

I remember one time after Dr. Odenwald's death, taking my clothes up to the cleaners. The owner of the dry-cleaning place had been a member of that pastor's church.

"It's very sad about Dr. Odenwald," I said.

"Yes," she said, "it is."

And she went on. "The last few Sundays," she said, "he'd been acting strange. He was talking about love and concern, but in a sad way."

So it was strange to hear all that talk about love and concern. So sad, I thought.

Are love and concern really as rare as all that?

The Whole Gospel

The next couple of years, '65 through '67, it seemed like we really needed Dr. Odenwald. And his "love and concern." Civil rights movements were really getting going, but too often in the wrong directions.

Malcolm X was shot and killed. James Meredith was shot on a voter registration march. Shot, but he marched on.

Riots and cattle prods. Deaths of whites and blacks. Action and reaction, spreading and growing. Chicago, Dayton, San Francisco, Watts.

Blacks were suddenly realizing and saying, "We are human!" And they were realizing it more suddenly than the whites were. Laws came up and went down and round and round. Laws to twist "equal" and "freedom" into "nice" and "stay put."

One history writer counted 'em up: "By 1964 Mississippi's massive resistance laws encompassed some forty statutes, solutions, and amendments. . . . Mississippi had the South's most formidable legal barriers to desegregation."[1]

I went to many civil rights rallies and talked with a lot of the people. I was an evangelical Christian, and our Voice of Calvary Bible Institute was growing. Our young people in Bible school and college were gaining a political and economic awareness, and a spiritual awareness.

But going to those political meetings, I could feel in my bones there was going to be trouble. Rioting and burning and trouble.

Why? Because issues were being raised. Valid issues. But they were being raised in and by groups that were not primarily evangelical.

The contribution of the civil rights movement to the black man's struggle for justice and equality is one that is undeniably great. And this is so, because those who led the movement were committed men and women. They were committed to the cause. And to the struggle.

But how sad that so few individuals equally committed to Jesus Christ ever became a part of that movement. For what all that political activity needed—and lacked—was spiritual input. Even now, I do not understand why so many evangelicals find a sense of commitment to civil rights and to Jesus Christ an "either-or" proposition.

One of the greatest tragedies of the civil rights movement is that evangelicals surrendered their leadership in the movement by default to those with either a bankrupt theology or no theology at all, simply because the vast majority of Bible-believing Christians ignored a great and crucial opportunity in history for genuine ethical action. The evangelical church—whose basic theology is the same as mine—had not gone on to preach the *whole* gospel.

So I decided to act, and this placed me squarely between two camps. I knew, of course, that we wouldn't get anywhere unless we started with the gospel that calls men to Christ for forgiveness and God's strength. For man cannot create justice by human manipulation alone. But at the same time, the Church, by so-called "spiritual" manipulation alone, cannot effect justice.

This thinking didn't all come at once. Back in California, when I first got saved, I right away got into a lot of action. I started Bible studies, training classes, child evangelism programs and other activities. I wasn't shutting out society's ills. I was suddenly seeing how much else there was to do and learn.

But now in 1965, civil rights issues were heating up. And everybody, black and white, had to take a stand. Besides, I wasn't just an evangelist anymore. I was involved with a growing institution. So I had to stand up and be counted, too.

Still, I had a Bible institute I was responsible for. And young people trying to get into colleges. Things like that.

I did a lot of thinking. By this time, we in Voice of Calvary were working with people of all ages. Vera Mae had begun a child-care center in 1964. And in 1966, with some added funds to help, it became a Head Start program.

I had several Bible classes of teens myself. I had seen so many family problems that I wanted to make sure that these kids didn't just get some isolated "religion," but also get some solid under-pinnings for family life as well. You will understand what I mean here about family life when I tell you that Vera Mae and I are the first generation of Perkins since slavery ever to stay together as a family. Our children, and the children we work with, now have a model, an example—something that I never had—for building healthy families of their own.

Each young person needed to know, first of all, who he is, know that he is a person. And know that, because he is a person, he is worth something. This is important, because, besides having and establishing their own families someday, they were going to have to find their own places in the growing excitement over political and economic issues already developing around us.

But besides the children and the teenagers, I saw that adults were also getting involved. They had their own Bible classes. And they provided support for the young people's activities. Things like that.

I could see that integration activities were certainly going to bring a lot of new money and help to the black community. But I did not feel that the mental breadth and spiritual stamina for success were there. You see, the problems we faced in the black community were primarily problems of values as well as structures.

Two-hundred years of slavery, followed by two or three generations of economic exploitation, political oppression, racial discrimination and educational deprivation, had created in black people feelings of inferiority, instability and total dependency. The implanting of such negative values in a people deprives them of any true sense of self-worth, or any real sense of self-identity. And the end result of negative values is negative behavior that is self-destructive in its effect. Dehumanizing values only and always produce destructive behavior.

So I could see that integration, equal opportunity, welfare, charity and all other such programs would in themselves fail to deal with the deep-seated values that had left our black communities spiritually bankrupt. Revolution—spiritual revolution, not reform or welfare—is the only solution to spiritual bankruptcy. And that is why the gospel of Jesus Christ, with its power to transform people by the renewing of their minds (see Rom. 12:2) is of primary importance to the black community.

At the same time, while observing the white evangelical church community, I was beginning to see that these white folks I had come to identify with religiously were going to have to deal with me in terms of social concern as well. I couldn't turn from that concern. I couldn't leave that out.

You see, the problem I saw was not entirely a "black problem." White people, too, have failed to allow the gospel to speak fully to them, to lifestyles and behavior patterns that are often exploitive and unjust. If Christ is Savior, He must also be Lord—Lord over such areas as spending, racial attitudes and business dealings. The gospel must be allowed to penetrate the white consciousness as well as the black consciousness.

But then, things are never as simple as we think. And I found that out right soon. For instance, I knew of a Bible institute for blacks and some other "missionary" projects where the blacks had made their adjustment to the Southern way of life and weren't interested in any push for political or economic equality. In other words, they weren't interested in anything that would rock their boat.

So, as we at Voice of Calvary began voter education and got involved in voter registration work, these blacks began pulling away from us. They had an easier way of life in the white missionary community, and it seemed their feelings of being real persons hung on that way of life. Anything that was different, anything that expected them to be persons on their own seemed to frighten them. It was almost like they still lived in the old plantation days.

So these "don't rock the boat" black Christians had to look down on the rest of the black community. There was no other way they could keep their secondhand personal identity. And the saddest part of it was that this attitude kept them from ever being able to bring the gospel of Jesus Christ to the black community they claimed to be so concerned about.

Whites did not reject my natural hairdo and beard as often as did these evangelical blacks who had made their peace with the status quo. To them, my beard was a sign of apostasy. So I shaved off the beard. I didn't depend on things like that. But voter education and voter registration had to go on.

In the tensions of those times, some of the civil rights workers who came south and who had no particular Bible background did turn to drinking for relaxation. And some of the younger women with no religious convictions had a casual attitude toward sex. So in some evangelical churches around the country, it became common to cite lurid reports of workers engaged in binges or orgies and then use these to argue that all civil rights activity was "godless" and should be condemned.

Now really. Let's see how that kind of thinking looks if we use it on some other activity, like business. Suppose a local store owner is not a Christian. He drinks too much, or cheats on his wife maybe. But when church people see that, do you hear them saying that business and private enterprise are "godless" and "of the devil"?

No. And especially not when the person is having a good sale on. What they say instead is that he could run his life and his business better, if he'd do so in a Christian way. *His basic work is approved*—they only say he ought to be cleaned up from some of the pagan ways he handles himself.

So with civil rights activity. Surely the job of working for justice is at least as important as being a good businessman. But how many calls did we hear in the '60s for *Christian* civil rights activity from those evangelicals who promoted such other things as Christian businessmen, Christians in entertainment, or Christian athletes? There are obviously immoral men and women in all those fields, but that doesn't cause church people to reject those activities as they did the movement for human justice. So all the focus on the questionable conduct of some—and only *some*—civil rights workers was, as I see it, just a pretext to avoid getting involved, an excuse to avoid the crying question: What should the Church do—what should I do—for the cause of human justice?

So I prayed that more Christians with real evangelical, Bible convictions would come. Not just to help with voter registration and such, but also to be a testimony to the bigness of the Bible—to how it takes in the whole person, both an individual's personal actions *and* social actions.

Each year I would visit the churches in California that were supporting our work. Here, too, some of my black evangelical friends were not interested in what was going on. They had a measure of personal satisfaction and economic opportunity in their own lives and weren't interested in problems of inequality and injustice outside that personal circle.

I talked to these blacks about other blacks that were trapped in a closed system that was quite different from theirs, but they were afraid of getting involved. Still, I talked to them about a lot of things—voter registration, for instance.

Where the political, social, economic and legal institutions are dominated by whites, inequities are inevitable. Voter registration was just one way that blacks hoped to be a part of those institutions that controlled their lives. Whites in the South had been so used to running things that even this voter activity— assumed as a natural right by people in other areas—seemed to Southern whites like dangerous radicalism. I told my California friends about my home county, Simpson County, where before there had been only 50 registered black voters. Then in one summer registration drive we got more than a thousand registered. And we finally ended up with more than 2,300.

This chance to live a whole, full life in the South was very important to those of us who had to do the living. But people outside the Southern trap sometimes viewed our activities with suspicion. Some of my white supporters thought I was using my time and their money for something different from their idea of "religion." There were comments like, "The whole idea of you going back there was to get people saved. Don't you think you are getting away from that?" Like I say, I did a lot of thinking. Salvation, of course, was both the foundation and the goal and everything in between. Or was it? What did the Bible mean by "brothers in Christ"?

I really wanted to share with others what Christ had been doing for me. Surely it wasn't God who was incomplete here. Surely we could see the same sort of real persons growing here. Maybe evangelical Christians, black and white, were confusing theology with the status quo.

It almost seemed at times like God was being packaged and handed out by a frightened alien system. It seemed to me that some of the institutions, supposedly promoted for helping blacks, actually contributed to the cycle of dependency. A Bible school, founded and run by white Southerners who were able to get other Southerners to help train the "poor, pitiful black people for the gospel," was, of course, not interested in anything that would be a challenge to the status quo.

In the eyes of blacks in the civil rights movement, both Christian and non-Christian, such "bought" or "tampered with" blacks simply couldn't express what was going on in the South. It wasn't so much that they had a different solution. They didn't even admit we had a problem.

So some of our support did dry up. In speaking engagements in both black and white churches I would try to defuse some of the standard objections. I could usually see them coming. For instance, if a questioner asked, "What do you think of Martin Luther King?" I knew where that question was leading.

So I would tell him, "You know, I lived in Mississippi. I grew up in Mississippi. I used to ride in those segregated buses—sit in the back of the bus. That's dehumanizing. When I would go to a restaurant someplace and would have to go round back, in all those dark dirty places, that would hurt. I saw people with hardly enough to eat, and knew of a lot who were killed—not because they had done anything wrong, but just because they were black."

I would tell them things like that, things they knew were still going on. They had to admit that these things were bad. We didn't usually get around to discussing King's theology, because they could guess that I would probably ask, "Well, what are you doing to correct these bad things with your 'good' theology?"

Usually the question would shift over to, "But you don't agree with violence, do you?"

"Violence? I don't believe that, overall, black folks believe in violence. Most black folks have been living in a state of violence in Mississippi and the South under conditions of white supremacy and segregation. Yet I don't know of one black person in Mississippi who has killed whites because of the situation."

Then I would remind them, "Violence, in relation to civil rights activities, is simply not a production of black people. Violence is a reaction of whites to black people who want nothing more than their freedom."

While that soaked in I would go on.

"In my activities, in my work, I don't even consider the question of violence. I'm not thinking on that level at all. I think on the basic level of freedom.

"Of course, there are some blacks who have got a lot of newspaper coverage because of violence. As a Christian I believe that all men are sinners, and that includes blacks who are also capable of turning against their fellow men.

"But in the overall history, in the social structure of black-white relations, it's a different story. The worst violence is the violence against blacks. That is *the* violence—violence that usually is accepted so nicely within the white system that it gets no publicity at all.

"The fact is that there are many more whites who believe in violence, or who believe in ignoring it when whites do it. But the black is always the person who gets asked about violence."

I said what I felt needed to be said, but I just stated facts as I saw them. I never severed ties, never cut off communication with anyone willing to talk. Because, you know, love is a giant thing if the person who has the complaint will not break the relationship.

This thing kept growing. I kept seeing new things that needed to be done. Like this waking up the middle-class evangelical church to responsibilities. Some evangelicals did not argue directly with me. They merely felt uncomfortable with me and just hoped I would disappear—without their having to suggest it.

This conflict around 1965 through 1967 was not a battle with myself about what I believed. I knew that the Bible commands us to seek justice. I had already thought that through and had come to firm conclusions.

But there were, and always will be, human emotions. Such as sadness at seeing those that I knew as brothers in Christ insist on a Sunday religion that didn't sharpen their sense of justice during those years of turmoil. It wasn't a question of what "team" to join. In terms of social justice, *evangelicals just didn't have a team on the field.*

And the sadness came in from the other directions, too. I had to watch ardent civil rights activists who could see the social inequities, but who left God out of the picture and thereby ignored the basic spiritual needs that existed. Still, I decided that if something was right, I would do it as a command from God and not be scared out because some non-Christians also thought it was right.

But I kept on longing for the day when it would be Christians in the forefront, taking seriously the words of the prophet Amos:

Take away from me the noise of your songs;
to the melody of your harps I will not listen.
But let justice roll down like waters,
and righteousness like an ever-flowing stream (5:23, *RSV*).

A typically discouraging example of religion "pulled into its shell" developed in the fall of 1966. That fall two of my children, Spencer and Joanie, along with six others, became the first black students in Mendenhall's previously all-white public high school. At the same time, there was an evangelistic effort through the school chapel program, causing many white young people to make a public profession of faith, in several different meetings. But walking down the aisle in a religious meeting, to announce a new life in Christ, apparently could not induce anyone to even step across an aisle at school to greet or get to know a lone black student.

For two years Spencer and Joanie walked through lonely halls. During those two years no white person would sit down with them. No white student ever held any conversation with them. And no student, teacher or adult religious leader in the white community, was willing to admit the wrongness of this situation.

I had to just watch. It hurt. The question kept popping up inside me: Does the gospel—that is, the gospel as we presently preach it—have within itself the power to deal with racial attitudes? The thing that hit me was that the supposed presence of the gospel was simply not effective in terms of human relations. If evangelism is truly on the side of God and His love, then it should never allow itself to look like it's on the side of a bigot-producing system.

After two years of that kind of pressure, we sent Spencer and Joanie to California for one semester. Then they both returned home—Spencer enrolling in the black high school and Joanie at Piney Woods, a private black school close by.

In 1970 a comprehensive integration program was instituted in Mendenhall by court order.

Note

1. Neil R. McMillan, "The Development of Civil Rights: 1956-1970," *A History of Mississippi*, ed. Richard Aubrey McLemore, vol. 2 (Hattiesburg University College Press of Mississippi, 1973), p. 156.

Taking a Stand

Thanks to the "Mississippi Plan," a smaller percentage of Mississippi's blacks were eligible to vote for president in 1964 than were eligible to vote for William McKinley way back in 1896.

The Mississippi Plan was the skeleton of the state's 1890 constitution, adopted that year by the Mississippi Constitutional Convention. It caused the surrender of political gains blacks had won through the Fourteenth and Fifteenth Amendments to the U.S. Constitution and the Civil Rights Act of 1870.

The new state constitution embodying the Mississippi Plan, and a lot of other legislation that followed, gave the lie to the refrain that "the way things were" after the war was just the survival of time-honored customs.

Over the post-reconstruction years, in elections in which racial demagoguery was the best vote getter, white politicians vied with each other to pour fresh ideas and programs into the old wineskins of prejudice. So Jim Crow laws—as well as the unlegislated customs—were, on the whole, new creations. They had to be newer than the "radical" post-Civil War laws directed toward Negro rights, for they were attempts made—*after* the laws—to invalidate them.

The Mississippi Plan outlined the requirements for voting. It did not mention Negroes, specifically. But it was easily administered by local officials to disenfranchise almost all Negro voters, and some white voters as well, without opportunity for appeal. The poll tax and literacy tests were the whites' best weapons. And the fact that blacks often had trouble with the white-run legal system also provided room for highly selective use of the clause that eliminated all those "convicted of bribery, theft, arson, obtaining money or goods under false pretenses, perjury, forgery, embezzlement or bigamy."

The poll tax seemed like a simple enough thing. Yet it was a barrier not only to the impoverished Negro without two dollars, but also to other blacks who would find that the local sheriff, doubling as tax collector, simply refused to accept their money.

The literacy requirement provided that the applicant fill out detailed personal information forms. He also should be able to read and write any section of the constitution of the state and give a reasonable interpretation of the section to the county registrar. The applicant also should demonstrate a reasonable understanding of the duties and obligations of citizenship under a constitutional form of government.

A possible section for interpretation that an applicant could be given at the discretion of the registrar might be Section 182, for instance:

The power to tax corporations and their property shall never be surrendered or abridged by any contract or grant to which the state or any political subdivision thereof may be a party, except that the legislature may grant exemption from taxation in the encouragement of manufacturers and other new enterprises of public utility extending for a period of not exceeding five years, the time of such exemptions to commence from date of charter, if to a corporation; and if to an individual enterprise, then from the commencement of work; but when the legislature grants such exemptions for a period of five years or less, it shall be done by general laws, which shall distinctly enumerate the classes of manufacturers and other new enterprises of public utility entitled to such exemptions, and shall prescribe the mode and manner in which the right to such exemptions shall be determined.

Still, in spite of all the roadblocks stacked in front of would-be black voters—including violence—black groups kept right on working for greater registration under then-existing rules of the state constitution. And because people all over the country were finding out about these obstructionist goings-on, the Mississippi legislature finally had to change some of the voting requirements. Then in several federal civil rights acts, including one in 1966, further barriers were struck down.

Although some of the legal handcuffs had been removed, it didn't take long to see that local officials were still dragging their feet, so federal voting registrars were sent into some areas. They were not exactly overwhelmed with local white cooperation. Sometimes they would scour the country for weeks without turning up any building, storefront or office that they could rent.

So, in Mendenhall, as in other towns, they wound up on the one piece of federal property, the Post Office. The loading dock of the Mendenhall Post Office still has the marks of the studwork and plywood that was nailed up to make a sort of outdoor office where blacks could come to register. These marks may not seem like big stuff to whites, like, say, an old slave auction block. But to blacks who remember the struggle for a simple right—the right to vote—they bring up the same kind of feelings.

Along with the federal registrars, civil rights workers of every kind, from white college students to our local groups from meetings held at Voice of Calvary, scattered out among the people.

In 1966, besides our regular work, we began voter registration and voter education activities. We went everywhere—to small towns and farms to talk, to give information, to persuade—and to stand by the fearful.

We started in Simpson County where we lived, and worked out from there to Smith County, Jeff Davis County, Copiah and Rankin Counties. In most places, I didn't need any introduction. This was where I had picked cotton, and now it was where I had school projects and Bible clubs. I was born and brought up here, and now it was my home again. Whites might call me "uppity," but they couldn't very well call me an "outside agitator."

Work at the loading dock of the Mendenhall Post Office, and at other voter registration points, went on through the heat of the '66 summer and on through 1967 and 1968. It wasn't a rush of black registration, but it was steady.

Local issues were often more worrisome than national issues, because the whites could see shifts of power coming in places like, say, the highway commission. Mississippi was divided into three highway districts: northern, southern and central. Jackson, the state capital, was just over the boundary in the central district. Mendenhall and the five counties I had worked in were in the southern district. The Southern District Commissioner, John D. Smith, who had held his post for 20 years, was noted as an outspoken racist. I happened to live right in his hometown.

The post of commissioner, besides offering personal prestige and political connections, was a pretty good patronage setup for hiring and firing highway department employees. In his 20 years as commissioner, John Smith hadn't given in to any of the pressure to integrate the highway department. Blacks just were not employed.

In 1968, a former school teacher and machinery salesman named William "Shag" Pyron opposed Smith. During the campaign he suggested that some of us blacks come talk with him. We did, and he let us know that it was about time blacks got employment in the highway department. If elected, he would see to that.

Now I can't say for sure what Pyron personally felt about blacks. I can't speak for him. But in this election, with just these two candidates, we supported Pyron.

The election troubled the white Establishment. The massive increase in black registered voters threatened to upset the system. And I was one of the most visible upsetters in my area. The tension in Mendenhall had plenty of spokesmen—anonymous voices over the phone:

"Perkins is a trouble-maker. He could get himself killed."

"Mrs. Perkins, you don't want to be a widow, do you?"

"Rev. Perkins is as good as dead right now. You better get out of town fast."

And cars began appearing at night. White men—armed, waiting. Watching for hours at a time, but edging closer and closer. Waiting for any incident to excuse a confrontation. Playing a war of nerves, not open warfare.

Finally, one Sunday afternoon about five o'clock, I went out into the community to talk to my people about the situation. By eight o'clock the church was packed with people. They agreed—something had to be done. So a volunteer guard group was formed.

From that night on—every night till the election—our house was guarded from dusk to dawn by armed men.

They sat or stood about the grounds, wrapped in the blanket of darkness—watching, listening and hoping that dawn would end another uneventful night. The only sounds they hoped to hear were the code words that signaled the approach of their relief, or maybe of one of the women bringing coffee and cookies to the men on duty.

Although hostility still showed up in other parts of Mendenhall, the regular guards around our house did have one visible effect: the Klan types who had kept their silent vigil soon disappeared. Klan-type mentality is not oriented toward open warfare; it is oriented toward control.

Acts of Klan violence were against black individuals for the purpose of keeping the black community under control, of scaring them back into line. The Klan only wanted to "teach a lesson," not wipe out a group. So organized opposition to Klan-type terrorism could be more effective here than in a "race war" or a mob-violence situation. Race riots and mob action can occur near city ghetto areas because each side sees the other as a different "nation," with warfare as a possible means of dealing with "them."

But in the different social situation of the rural South, the Klansman and his spiritual kin, as often as not, have regular dealings with the blacks. He might be a small store owner, for instance. Blacks might owe him money, or he might depend on blacks—and his sense of control over them—in other ways. So, to him, blacks are a part of his world. They are within his system and frame of reference in a way unknown to most white city dwellers.

The Southern white doesn't want the blacks *removed*. What he wants is to have the blacks under his control, in a special relationship to him. So one of the greatest sins in the eye of the typical Southern racist is for someone to take away control of "his" niggers.

The election. Pyron defeated the incumbent, Smith, and the black votes were significant in his victory. So, for the first time, he opened up some highway jobs for blacks.

The election encouraged blacks in the area. But the whole agonizing process of court litigation, voter registration and voter education had effects that spilled beyond the actual election process. True, they had seen their own candidate for office elected. They had seen the importance of influencing the course of their own history.

But more than that, they had taken a stand for the first time. And this had already had great positive effect on the self-image of many blacks conditioned never to have their hopes very high. Now their hopes soared along with a rising sense of their own self-worth. And not just because they had voted and won. But because they had taken a stand.

In situations of inequality or oppression, the oppressed group *must* take a stand somewhere, sometime. For until the people take that stand, there is no development possible for them. Yet when they take that stand in the face of clear injustice, an oppressed people are once again humanized. And they then become capable of a level of development—spiritual, economic, social or other—not psychologically possible for a people still in a passive, dependent state.

Some writers on revolution—especially in the Third World with its exposure to international colonialism—say "taking a stand" has to be done by "taking up the gun" against the oppressor. Yet even when opposed to that particular kind of armed revolution, it is still possible to agree with the psychological and spiritual truth behind it: the necessity for and importance of taking a stand in the face of injustice. But the right kind of "revolt"— if we want to call it that—is an absolute must. Yet too many white church people do not recognize that. They teach their own sons to "stand up and be a man," teach them to be confident. Then they go all to pieces when an oppressed minority starts doing just that.

Of course, how that act takes place is important, but the declaring of a people's manhood has to be an act. For some of our people the beginnings of that act reached back over several years. For many others, it was focused in that election year, 1968.

It was no coincidence, therefore, that 1968 was also the official beginning of the Leadership Development Program at Voice of Calvary. Of course we had been developing leaders from the beginning. But that year we organized a definite program of integrating young leadership into each project. We had always encouraged young people to finish high school and go off to college. Now some of these young people were beginning to come back for the summer, or to look for new direction.

These young people were especially useful in the summer tutoring program and in conducting Bible classes for younger students. And the learning was a two-way street. They were not only learning how to do things, but even more basic, they learned why these things needed to be done.

Between 1939 and 1964, more than two million blacks had left the deep South. The already crushing problems in the Southern black communities now were aggravated further by the leadership gap, with black populations too heavily concentrated in the very old and the very young groups. Our Leadership Training Program was one grassroots effort saying to the would-be emigrants, "You are needed here. You can have a meaningful life here."

Cooperatives Are the Key

As I said, I did a lot of thinking in the late '60s. Sometimes I would think back to my childhood. And when I did, I saw my life pattern as a repeated theme—a fight to escape from an economic system that enslaves.

Even among evangelicals, I seemed to be seeing the same thing I had tried to escape from all my life. I began wondering then about matters that later led to things like co-ops for the powerless and penniless. And since my ideas about co-ops were rooted deep in my theology, they had entirely unique goals. They would be more than just an economic escape from the old plantation system whose ghost still haunted us.

So alongside the voter activities of the mid '60s, I found another positive focus for activity: economic cooperatives. Several other organizers of the rural poor saw the co-op movement as providing a mechanism for self-development that would produce more than financial advances. It could provide activity and training for people used to having things done for them, and so start them out of this cycle of dependence.

One such worker was Father A.J. McKnight, a black Roman Catholic priest who eventually left his pulpit for full-time administration of economic activities. He had obtained a Ford Foundation grant to help form co-ops in the South. I went to hear McKnight speak, and knew right away that co-ops could answer some of the problems we faced in Simpson County.

So a couple of months later, in September 1967, I attended a workshop held in Abbeyville, Louisiana, sponsored by the Southern Educational Foundation, McKnight's group. I listened and talked and thought. These were people with high economic motivation.

As a Christian, I felt I was catching on to a *solution* to a problem that we faced. Co-ops fit into my theological understanding. But I could see that the strain on my evangelical friends was going to be tough, because they didn't have any framework to deal with economics from a Christian perspective.

Yet as I looked at my brothers and sisters at the conference, and knew the tension that economics would create, I wondered whether we who were there had the spiritual strength to meet the challenge. A spiritual lack was felt at the workshop, though they didn't feel that Christianity—at least as they knew it—had any real answers. One resource person for the conference, who was a business consultant for *Ebony* magazine and a successful urban black, looked across the spectrum of new economic activities in the nation's black communities, and admitted to me that unless there was "quick and fervent" spiritual activity in the black community, it could destroy itself with the new economic push. He agreed that the economic fabric—that is, the general attitudes such as the honesty of black folks—was no stronger than what the white structure had. And he, with the others at the workshop, saw the white economy as hypocritical and too often geared toward selfishness and monopoly. Was this what we were trying to be a part of?

I began to see that the average strength of Christian understanding in the black community was too weak to carry the burden of the businessman. The emotional worship typical of many parts of the black church since Emancipation often lacked real Bible content. But you can't really criticize it until you understand what it did, and still does, for us as people. It was a strain to live in a world where you were "free," but still didn't have any real control over important parts of your life, over matters that affected you and your community. The black minister who had some skill in drawing out or transferring that strain and emotion helped maintain the sanity and mental health of a people suffering and oppressed.

But other needs were not met, such as the need for economic development, so important today. And, of course, that worship was not directed toward the mind or the understanding. I think hypertension among blacks is related to this vacuum between two worlds—one the heavenly, beautiful, spiritual world; the other the harsh, brutal, real world of economics.

Take the black businessman, the black man who has maybe gone to college and has rejected the black emotional church because he doesn't see enough intelligence in it. And he really has not been exposed to the central truths of the gospel. So what we have is one of the world's largest, untouched mission fields—right here in this country. And because the field is untouched, we see a few blacks becoming a comfortable part of the white man's success bag, and a majority suffering the strain of living in an unjust environment without the spiritual dynamics of knowing Christ.

At that conference I began to see the usefulness of co-ops as a tool in helping to bring humanity to blacks. So I helped to organize the Federation of Southern Co-ops, dedicated to development of local resources and local income. That was near the end of 1967.

The 1960 census classified only one-third of the housing units for blacks in Mississippi as "sound." The remaining two-thirds were described as "dilapidated" or "deteriorating." So I felt that housing was the place for us to begin our first co-op effort in Mendenhall. I felt that a successful housing co-op would have effects far beyond the actual provision of better housing, important as that was. It could provide a vital break from the cycle of despair and feelings of ineffectiveness, a break that could be mobilized in a continuing spiral toward other goals.

The first stage was just the time-consuming work of talking to tenants living in $15-a-month housing. That was the first problem. Even by the most modest estimates and utilization of co-op efforts, I figured a decent house would cost occupants about $60 a month. A solid, real brick house with plumbing.

So over the months I worked this project into other activities and found some families willing to officially organize a co-op for housing. At first we talked about building some self-help units. We could hire a contractor to put up a basic structure, and the owners would then put in "sweat equity," finishing the interior themselves.

But the people willing to join the co-op in the first place were not the unemployed. They were already working—many of them long hours, and that would stretch out the whole timetable into an unknown infinity of part-time picking away at the problem.

Then we learned of federal help available through the Farmers' Home Administration—not to be confused with the other "FHA," the Federal Housing Authority. I fired off some letters to Washington as well as to local offices. Many government offices at that time had the funds and the mandate to fund positive projects that would help the poor and the politically dispossessed. And here we were with the local leadership and a local organization that could help carry the ball.

The time was ripe! Hardly a couple of weeks later federal officials showed up at my house with a black official who was to work with our own co-op and help carry it through. This was the first black FHA man in our county.

With the funds from the local members and an $84,000 loan from the FHA, we began the construction of 10 duplex units. They were owned by the local co-op, which managed the funds and became the collective landlord of those who would pay rent into the loan retirement fund. In the summer of 1969 the first family moved in.

Although the co-op has not built more houses since, I regard this venture as highly successful. For one thing, the idea from the beginning was not to provide everyone around with a co-op house. Rather, the co-op was the only way in the economically depressed area to take the first significant steps toward better homes and eventually toward home ownership for everyone.

That first step was necessary for many more reasons than the obvious one of providing better housing for some. I and a lot of other people who take a good look at the poverty problem are pretty dissatisfied with the typical aid, poverty or welfare program. Too often such programs have simply channeled money through the hands of recipients back to merchants without having a lasting, organic effect on the ability of the community itself to deal with its problems.

In order to combat the cycle of discouragement, ignorance and exploitation, it seems to me there is a basic need for indigenous organizations and communities whose life substance feeds on local efforts, local training and local leadership. Many people with politically conservative attitudes agree with this in the sense that they say, "Federal handouts don't help. People themselves must be their own economic salvation." And then they vote for further reduction of funds.

But, actually, this is only the top skimming of what I see. It doesn't touch the basics. It is true that money alone doesn't solve problems. But few people understand or realize how truly dependent even the most rugged individualist is on others.

No person, no group that has achieved middle- or upper-class status, has *really* done it all alone. There has always been a resource input, and without that input even the firmest determination can get nowhere. So the debate that circles around such issues may be as pointless as the old chicken-or-the-egg controversy; you can't pinpoint what comes first, but they are both necessary. When we look at the poor getting poorer through the self-perpetuating cycle of ignorance, poor health and lack of opportunity, two truths are evident: (1) money must be made available to develop potential, and (2) the community itself must develop its potential to utilize and multiply economic resources. When programs are totally designed by the helpers, the helpees (to coin a term) don't always get much help.

So, with an eye on the overall goal of indigenous community vitality, our housing project looked like a way of bringing economic awareness right into the black home. The black community had little economic understanding, no investment education. So the co-op was a school as well as a provider.

Getting people into their own homes was one practical answer to the question of developing personal responsibility and competence. For instance, the black FHA representative did much more than handle some of the technical paperwork. He spoke at meetings in the church and community. He helped the local board in the development of their record-keeping and supervisory responsibilities. He helped people who knew nothing about individual FHA loans. In fact, one heartening result is that more private individuals actually built their own homes backed by FHA loans, uplifting the entire community.

Where I lived and worked, this project was an *economic* responsibility. But it was also a *Christian* responsibility. There are many instances of this dual responsibility in the Bible besides the familiar story of the Good Samaritan. The first letter of John, a very "spiritual" epistle, has some obvious commands about how our faith should show in active help for the physical needs of others (see 1 John 3:16-18; also Matt. 25:31-46).

I want all people to come to know Jesus Christ. Nothing I do takes the place of that. But I wonder if, maybe, someone in the Billy Graham organization or some other evangelical organization had discovered the polio vaccine, would they have given it only to the Christians, or to everybody? I bet they would probably have given it to everybody.

But why is it then that some Christians get all hot under the collar when an organization like ours gets out and helps the whole community? I see economic education as a total responsibility to all people. And that responsibility is not lessened if some of those helped do not respond to our preaching of the gospel.

With the visible success of the housing co-op, it became less difficult to organize other co-ops. While the first families were moving into the co-op houses in 1969, many farmers were feeling the economic pinch as supplies, such as fertilizer, kept going up in price. With their livelihood already marginal, there was little room left to absorb extra costs.

So we got the farmers' co-op off the ground with the necessary organization and record-keeping setup. That year the farmers' co-op bought more than 200 tons of fertilizer directly from the wholesale distributor in Brookhaven, Mississippi. Some co-op members bought only a few bags, others 20 or more tons, at savings of $6 to $12 a ton.

Such a business operation was not as publicly visible as, say, the voter registration activities and did not attract as much attention from white merchants who might have resented the newly formed operation. One day, when a 75-ton shipment was being unloaded, a retail dealer who was losing the business did come down to watch, but nothing came of that. The fertilizer was stored in the warehouse section of a cement block building that was to become the next co-op operation, the co-op store.

Whatever we did, we just had to go along on what we saw was needed. We had no way of guessing ahead of time what the reaction of the whites would be. And to tell you the truth, we couldn't afford to care.

Actually, there weren't enough communication channels open at the time between whites and blacks to know who was thinking what. For instance, I was talking one time to a well-to-do white businessman who was considering a donation to the Voice of Calvary ministries, and he asked what the local white Christians thought of our work. I told him that I just didn't know.

I couldn't know. Because I, a black man, was just as unwelcome in white churches as in white non-Christian organizations and homes. I said a decision would just have to be made on the merits of the project, not on possible reaction to it.

So the white churches remained silent. At least the black community didn't hear or know what they were saying. But we had been hearing other voices, threatening voices—though after the death threats of the 1968 election there had been fewer of these.

I went on with my pretty intensive schedule: the co-ops, the leadership training, the Bible classes and church activities. And in the white community, as our accomplishments grew, the resentment kept pace, building up emotion that sooner or later would find an excuse to explode.

Then, as 1969 drew to a close, whites and blacks alike began their usual—separate—preparations to celebrate the birth of the Prince of Peace.

Disturbing
the Peace

Christmas 1969 was only a couple of days away. It was just getting dark as Doug Huemmer and I drove down Main Street in Mendenhall, and holiday lights began to twinkle on all over the white part of town. Behind us, Christmas lights glowed on the town square and on the stately, domed county courthouse.

In front of us, Main Street and the rest of the Christmas lights sloped gently down to the highway on the white side of the railroad tracks that divided the white and black sections of town. Along the highway were businesses like the tractor sales place, the lumber yards and a Chevrolet agency.

Main Street was mostly stores—shops of all kinds. They lined both sides of the street and were all lighted up and decorated fancy with wreaths and tinsel for the holidays. Christmas music seemed to be everywhere, filling the air.

Silent night! Holy night—

We weren't driving fast. No way we could drive fast in that old, beat-up, Volkswagen we were using then.

All is calm, all is bright—

Along the highway outside Mendenhall were some signs. These sure were no Burma-Shave signs; still nobody coming into town could help seeing them—and reading them. Nor could I help thinking that the words of the carol that night sure had a different ring to them than the ones on those road signs: "White people unite, defeat Jew/Communist race mixers."

Round yon virgin mother and Child—

Doug and I were headed for the little grocery store not far down the highway from where it crossed Main Street. They have country cane syrup there, and Doug wanted to take some to his folks in Glendale, California, for Christmas. He was planning to fly home that evening, so he'd put in a hard day already, trying to get a lot of things finished before leaving.

Holy Infant, so tender and mild—

I saw Doug looking at his watch. It would soon be time to leave for the airport in Jackson. Good kid, Doug, sensitive, intelligent. He was one of the young white volunteers that came to help Voice of Calvary with the work that always seems to need doing as we keep growing. He had been with us longer than many of the volunteers and I hoped he had caught glimpses of the God who is the source of all real love, even though Doug wasn't giving Him much credit for it.

Sleep in heavenly peace—

Doug seemed to sort of loosen up a bit as the carols floated out to us from everywhere.

Sleep in heavenly peace.

I knew nobody in town would be surprised at seeing Doug and me together. Since Voice of Calvary already had a number of other white volunteers besides Doug, most of the local whites by this time had seen blacks and whites together. But they still hadn't gotten used to it.

So local white reaction was often cool and sometimes hostile. There was never any of the usual small talk with me, like "How are you today, Rev. Perkins?" You know, the sort of talk other blacks heard when they went into a store. It was like I spoke another language. Maybe I did.

It was almost dark as Doug and I turned down the highway and pulled up at the grocery. Inside the store, a young black man, Garland Wilks, was trying to pay by check for some stuff he bought. But he wasn't getting very far in convincing the white storekeeper to accept the check. Besides that he had been drinking. He wasn't drunk; just a little high. But he got madder and madder, and his voice got louder and louder.

We picked up Doug's syrup from a shelf and paid for it. And Garland—who was still yelling—was getting farther and farther away from the mandatory "Yessir." I could tell that the storekeeper and the other customers were getting annoyed. So I suggested to Garland that we give him a ride home.

It worked. Garland agreed. So Doug and I grabbed him and shoved him outside into our car. We jumped in after him and slammed the doors.

Whew! What a relief! That little ruckus in the store could easily have grown into an ugly incident.

But what I didn't know was that the angry grocer had already phoned the police. We were heading for Garland's house with Doug driving when a patrol car showed up behind us. I began to get a little tense. If you're black and in the South, that's a natural reaction.

The police tailed us across the railroad tracks and followed us along the paved streets onto the dirt road that led to the black section of town. We were just a few blocks from the Voice of Calvary when the patrol car switched on its blue flasher. We pulled over.

Doug hopped out of the car even faster than I did and asked the officer, "Is something wrong?"

"You just shut up! Stand aside!" one of the policemen yelled.

One of the officers leaned inside the open door of our VW and said, "Come out of there, Garland. You're under arrest!"

"Under arrest for what?" I asked.

"Public drunkenness and disturbing the peace."

Disturbing the peace! That handy catch-all charge.

"But he's in the car with us. He's not disturbing the peace."

The officer growled an oath and snarled, "You shut up!"

Garland was still in the car, and both Doug and I continued to protest. We promised to take Garland home ourselves.

"Just shut up!"

There was nothing more we could do. Garland came out of the VW and climbed into the patrol car. I told Doug, "You drive straight to Voice of Calvary. I'm going on down to where Garland's grandma lives and tell her what happened. Then I'll walk home from there." I promised Garland's grandma I would visit him in jail and see about his bail.

At VOC, our college students—home for the holidays—and local students were busy rehearsing a Christmas pageant. As I reached there, one of the girls, Carolyn Albritton (who later married Mendenhall Bible Church pastor Artis Fletcher), came out, and I told her what happened. She got sort of excited and began talking so fast I could hardly understand her at first. Finally I understood that just that afternoon over by her house, a boy, Roy Berry, had been arrested and badly beaten as he came out of church. But it wasn't until much later that anybody knew what Roy was supposed to have done.

"He ain't done nothin', Rev. Perkins," Carolyn said. "They claimed he was makin' phone calls to a white woman askin' her for a date, and they took him down to jail and beat him. They said they ought to kill him!"

Somebody or other had decided that Roy Berry was the guilty party. But nobody knew how or why. For now, all anybody knew was that a black boy had been grabbed and beaten by "the law." And now another one—Garland Wilks—had been arrested.

Carolyn burst into tears. "They gonna beat up Garland, too!" she kept saying.

I listened to Carolyn and believed what she was telling me. I'd lived through enough outbreaks of police brutality in Mendenhall to know the truth when I heard it. Ever since blacks had started agitating in the early '60s, white hatred had been rising and rising. Now it was finally spilling over, like water breaking through a dam. A rash of beatings and arrests had erupted. As one white man had told me to my face, "You gotta keep the nigger in his place."

The Christmas rehearsal broke up as both Doug and Mrs. Wilks arrived on the scene. I suggested we go and see what had happened to Garland. Then Doug and I took the whole group uptown to the police station in City Hall to ask about Garland. At the time, it seemed the wisest move to make. If I had gone alone, I'd probably be arrested and beaten myself. But 17 people of all ages, including junior high kids, surely would not be jailed. In fact, four of my own kids were in that nervous, noisy group of folk.

We rode together in about three cars uphill to the railroad tracks, across them, then turned right on Jackson Avenue, or old 49, and finally turned left and went up to the City Hall.

Stores were open late this last week before Christmas, and we passed cars filled with shoppers as we came toward town. We pulled into the parking lot of City Hall about two blocks from the courthouse and about a block and a half from the jail. The Mendenhall police force consisted of the chief and two or three deputies. The chief himself, Mark Sherman, met us out in the parking lot. One of the teenagers spoke up: "Did you beat Garland up?"

In response, the chief assured us, "We ain't laid a hand on him. There he is over there in the car." We looked over and Garland was still sitting in the back of the squad car.

"But you beat up my cousin, Roy Berry, this afternoon," the girl insisted.

Again the chief protested, "Our Mendenhall police had nothing to do with that case. The county sheriffs took that one. You'll have to go on over to the jail and see for yourself."

Some walked and some rode the block and a half to the Mendenhall jail. It was a typical small-town arrangement with no imposing staff or elaborate bureaucratic procedures for coming and going. The jailer and his family lived in the same building, and their front door opened off the jail's front entrance hall.

All 17 of us trooped into the jail building together, surprising and upsetting Mr. Griffiths, the jailer, and his wife. "We came to see Roy Berry," we told him. Our announcement seemed to unnerve the jailer even further.

Meanwhile, more people had joined us, waiting by their cars. And in the lobby of the jail, a debate took place, as our confrontation with the jailer continued. Chaos was building.

Griffiths walked into the booking office off the lobby. About 12 of us followed him. Now he was really getting scared. He said, "You're all under arrest." And he opened the big steel doors to the cell block.

If this was the only way we were going to see Roy, so be it. Doug stepped forward. The jailer grabbed him and shoved him through the door. I walked in behind him and everybody followed.

Slam! The door clanged shut as the jailer slammed it shut behind us, locked it and reminded us we were all under arrest. And then we realized—we'd just been locked in jail! About a dozen of us!

The jailer didn't quite know what was going on or what might happen next. But he was pretty sure he'd at least removed the threat that he had felt personally. So he immediately called the county sheriffs department and the Highway Patrol. They asked him who the demonstrators were. They soon found out: a minister, a white social worker and some innocent kids. And he had jailed the whole bunch of us without proper arrest and with no charges against us.

Without admitting he was wrong, the jailer came to the bars and asked the kids if they were ready to go. He'd let most of them off free, he said.

The kids, however, wanted an explanation of why they'd been locked up, but the jailer wasn't about to give them one. They argued back and forth for a while until the jailer went back to his desk. It was a stalemate until the Highway Patrol, the county sheriff and district attorney arrived.

And arrive they did. Their response to the jailer's call was immediate. And, you see, the state Highway Patrol had about doubled in size in 1964 when Mississippi claimed to fear mass disturbances in the wake of increased civil rights activities. Sworn testimony and other documents indicate that the Highway Patrol was something less than impartial. It had become a vicious, last-stand vigilante attempt to preserve the traditions of the closed society.

Civil rights lawyers had stated flatly that the increased force, without a proportionate increase in normal law enforcement needs, simply provided extra muscle for suppressing legal activities. So any call for help in a racial situation could count on a quick response from patrol cars—and that's what happened then when the Mendenhall jailer called for help.

At the same time, the others who had been outside the jail and who had not gotten in before the jail door slammed, went back to the church and told everybody there what had happened. Pretty quick a crowd of our people and folks from all over the county began to gather outside the jail.

The white officials hadn't planned on things happening quite this way, but once it was done they couldn't admit any mistakes. The only question for them now was how to best back up the actions of the jailer. So the Highway Patrolmen talked in hushed tones with the jailer for a while, and then offered us a proposal.

A large officer, chewing gum, approached the bars. "Tell you what, kids," he said. "If you leave nice and easy, nobody will be hurt. We just want to keep Rev. Perkins and this Huemmer fella overnight. But you kids better get out of here."

Nobody moved. It was no sale. The kids weren't buying the officer's proposal. One teenager announced, "We ain't goin' no place without Rev. Perkins and Doug. They didn't do anything we didn't do, too. So either turn us all out, or we all stay."

The others nodded their heads in agreement. The patrolman cursed and went back to the group of officers. They discussed what to do next with their "prisoners."

Meanwhile, more people had gathered around the front of the jail. Those of us inside could hear our people outside demanding explanations. Vera Mae was among the crowd, wondering along with the rest what was happening to me and the children inside.

You see, when I and the others had come to the jail to see what we could do about getting Roy out, Vera Mae had remained home with a friend, Rachel Brown. So she and Rachel were there at the house when Carolyn's sister, Martha Ann, came rushing in with our baby daughter and a couple of other children. "Mrs. Perkins," Martha Ann shouted, "Brother Perkins and your other kids and everybody's been locked up. The only reason I ain't been locked up too was they told me to bring these kids back home."

Vera Mae got on the phone and called some good friends of ours. But she couldn't call everybody; there weren't many telephones out there in the rural communities. So after phoning everybody she could, she had to wait for them to get in their cars and drive around to the houses of the president of the NAACP and some other folks. Then they all went up to the jailhouse together.

Brothers Isaac and Jesse Newsome were there. Mitchell Hayes and W.B. Langston were there. Uncle Archie Buckley was there. There were quite a few others out there with Vera Mae that night. I was glad later knowing she wasn't out there in the dark and cold all alone.

There wasn't a lot Vera Mae and the others could do when they got to the jailhouse except stand outside there in the dark, praying and crying and wondering what was happening inside. And since the jail was upstairs, they couldn't see in—just look up at the windows from below. But they could hear the children crying.

Vera Mae could hear our oldest daughter, Joanie, crying out to her. "Momma, they're beating up Daddy up here. And they broke Doug's glasses."

And some of the others were yelling out, "I'm going to smother up here."

"It's so dirty in here."

They were really carrying on.

But what to do next with us was a difficult problem for the authorities. If anything, the screams of the kids had attracted an even bigger crowd outside than before. But it wasn't the size of the crowd—important as that was—that made the situation a genuine crisis for the white officials. What made things so tense for them was the fact that the main black leadership of Simpson County was right there in that crowd outside the jail. I knew they were there, too. I had seen them from the window. And that made it sort of unhandy for any officers to beat me up; they managed that sort of thing only when they didn't have to explain to any onlookers.

Like I said before, the general attitude of the white power structure was the desire for control, not just antagonism. And whatever measure of control they had—or thought they had— could have been broken or strained by a total alienation of all blacks, especially those who were more disposed to cooperate with whites, the so-called "Uncle Toms." Since the "cooperative" blacks were all there in the crowd outside the jail as well as those not so cooperative, the police knew this was no time for "lesson teaching."

Out there in the crowd, Vera Mae herself wasn't sure what to do. She just knew she had to be there. She heard a white man—a patrolman—telling the blacks in the crowd that I was a false leader of my people, that I was misleading them and that they ought to turn against me. Actually, the circumstances just then weren't exactly ideal for his pitching that kind of line to the blacks standing there in the dark outside the jail where Doug and I were being held on no known charges. If anything, his words that evening only helped solidify us blacks in our distrust of the whites.

As she moved about through the crowd, Vera Mae noticed that the white speaker was a Highway Patrol member, Lloyd Jones, or "Goon" Jones as he had gotten himself nicknamed. Jones was talking to a local black minister about "all these rumors of violence inside." "Now really," Jones asked in his most polite voice, "do *you* think I'd do something like that?"

The minister quickly gave the "proper" reply, "No, sir, I don't."

Then turning, Jones saw Vera Mae and asked, "Do you think I would?"

"Yes, I do," she replied and turned away. Vera Mae was in no mood for this game of words.

From the jail window, I could hear the crowd of blacks below arguing my case amongst themselves. I knew this could go on all night. There was nothing I could do to help the situation. But was there nothing I could say?

I could feel a great churning inside me. But it wasn't anger I felt. It was anguish, pity, grief. Yes, and love. So deep and so strong, I couldn't contain it. It just filled me up and spilled out of me.

Through the bars of the window I started speaking to the crowd in the street below. I had to reach them somehow. I had to let them know I cared very much about them—about all of them. And they cared about me. But they were also angry—angry for me. And angry enough to do something about it.

I begged them not to do anything we would all regret. I warned them that if we gave in now to anger and violence and hate, we would be just like the whites. And we would be doing the very same things to them that they were doing to us. But they would be the winners, and we would be the losers.

We would gain nothing and lose everything. We hadn't gained a whole lot yet. But if we returned hate for hate, anger for anger and violence for violence, we would lose what little we had already gained along with any hope of ever gaining anything else.

I said all that—and a whole lot more. The power, the emotion of what I was saying that night was so great, I don't remember exactly all I did say. But I know my heart was in every word I spoke.

Even as I warned our people that we could only hurt ourselves seeking revenge, I reminded them that we could also hurt ourselves, and our children as well, if we simply caved in and did nothing. The legal system was making no effort at all for real justice for blacks. In fact, it was working against us.

That meant we had to take a stand ourselves. For ourselves. Someplace. Sometime. The place was here. And the time was now.

But I didn't want anymore suffering. And I didn't want to do anything to add to their suffering. They had suffered too much already. I told them—and I meant it—if somebody still had to suffer, I was willing. And if somebody had to die, I was ready.

But the truth was that nothing I did alone—whether I lived, suffered behind bars or died—would really make any difference. And nothing any of them did alone would make any difference. None of us could do it alone. All of us in the black community would have to pull together. We would have to take our stand together. And together we could do it. That's why we black folks needed each other at that moment more than ever before.

As I spoke, I prayed that they would feel even a little of what I was feeling for them just then, that they would understand what I was saying to them and why. I restated for them all the demands that we in the black community had been trying to bring to the attention of local officials. Like the fact that no blacks worked anywhere in uptown Mendenhall except as janitors, domestics and cooks. So we wanted better jobs for black people. And better living conditions. Paved streets and things like that. All we wanted was a better life for our people, for all people.

And then as I was speaking, the idea came to me of a boycott. An economic boycott! And why not? In a small town like Mendenhall, where the political and business interests were essentially the same, the idea of blacks staying away from the stores made a lot of sense.

Especially in Christmas week. Especially with a shopping rush going on.

The black community had put a lot of items on layaway until Christmas Eve. I asked everyone who had put items on layaway in town to leave them up there. And I asked everybody who could hear me to stop all buying and shopping in Mendenhall until the town started hurting. Then maybe when the whites were hurting, they would listen to us, hear us, and know how much we were hurting, too.

I said all that—and kept on talking. It seemed like a whole lifetime of feeling poured through me as I talked. Then I stopped. And waited.

The youngsters, of course, were still the touchiest problem for the police. They had provided a background of controlled chaos all during my "speech." So finally the officers decided to remove them by force from the jail, leaving only Doug and me. We were still under arrest, they said. So one by one, they carried out the teenagers and the younger kids. The kids were screaming their heads off, yelling, "No, no. I won't go."

And naturally, every parent outside at first, including Vera Mae, was sure that the screaming kid was their own, and that he was being beaten. Grabbing the kids by their arms and legs and lifting them bodily off the floor, the police finally got all of them pushed outside, leaving only Doug and me inside. Then the patrolmen sealed off the door and refused to let anyone else inside.

Around midnight, I guess, a young lawyer came to see Doug and me. James Robinson of the Lawyers' Committee for Civil Rights sent him down to us. He left later with the assurance that everything possible would be done for us.

Nothing more could be settled that night. So about two or three in the morning Doug and I were officially charged and locked up. What the exact terms of the charge were and when they were lodged were later disputed at the trial.

About the same time, the crowd outside the jailhouse—now very silent and almost frozen in the winter night air—broke up and headed home. The streets of Mendenhall were quiet at last. And Doug and I were officially in jail.

The cell was bare. And the floor was hard. No Christmas carols now—except in memory.

All is calm, all is bright—

I had trouble sleeping.

Green Power!

A lot of people in Mendenhall had trouble sleeping that night. And some weren't even trying. They were too busy doing other things. Like getting ready for a boycott.

After the lawyer had gone and the crowd around the jailhouse began to break up, Vera Mae—with the college students and the younger kids—went back home to Voice of Calvary. But hardly anybody went to bed. And there was little sleep.

Instead, they all went to the church building. They had to make plans. Somehow, in my suggesting a boycott, they all felt I had given them just what they needed to make it possible for the black man to stand up to the white man. But, angry as they were, they had sense to know—if they were going to make that boycott work—they needed some organization and strategy. And *that* I hadn't given them.

You see, this boycott thing wasn't planned at all. It came to our heads suddenly. Just like that. Everything had happened so fast in just a few hours, we hardly were ready to take a stand. But ready or not, we had to do it.

Vera Mae filled me in on what happened that night. Even while the kids talked, all noisy and nervous-like, they were already at work, busy making picket signs out of anything they could lay their hands on. They stayed up all night sawing up wooden slats, cutting up cardboard boxes, pasting down the cardboard and using up one Magic Marker after another writing the signs they would carry during the boycott.

Come sunup, the boycott was organized and ready to roll. And by eight o'clock that morning, Vera Mae and our kids from VOC were already up in the town, peacefully picketing the stores, quietly placing different persons at key areas on the street and announcing a total boycott of all businesses. And they made it clear the boycott would go on as long as necessary.

Vera Mae wasn't too sure at first what she should do herself. This boycott thing was new to her. But she felt she had to "lead out," so she stood on the street corner opposite the bank, right where cars with shoppers coming into town would slow to stop or turn.

If a car had blacks in it, she would go over to them and say, "We ain't shoppin' in Mendenhall this Christmas."

"Why, honey? What happened?" "Well. they got Brother Perkins and Doug in the jail for no reason, and ain't doin' nothin' about it. Go shop in Magee or Jackson, or somethin'."

This having to shop in other towns was hard for some people, because they had money already deposited on layaway items in Mendenhall. People were even willing to forfeit their money laid away on bicycles, sewing machines and other stuff. So as much as Vera Mae could see, cooperation of Mendenhall blacks was total. And other blacks from all over the county and outside counties cooperated with the boycott, too. They left.

Everybody cooperated. None of our people passed Vera Mae and went into any store. It made her feel kinda good. It meant the black community was pulling together. The black community was taking a stand. It was making an impact.

Not all of the black kids could afford to picket. Some had parents working in white homes. But those manning the picket lines knew the others were behind them. For while they picketed, the others were back at VOC cooking for them.

In fact, the boycott was working so good it surprised everybody. No black shoppers, and only a few whites, could be found on the streets. Just orderly groups of picketers manning positions at key points in the business district.

Blacks in town honored the boycott. That's why they stayed away. But when they saw the picketers up and down Main Street, most of the whites stayed away too.

Whites who don't want us in politics sure do need our business. No last minute Christmas shopping. No lay-away pickup. Day before Christmas, this boycott was bad news for a lot of store owners.

By 10 A.M. they could tell how bad things really were. Frustrated storekeepers pressured the police and town officials to do something, anything to get rid of the Perkins case. The sheriff came to me and pleaded for me to make bond and get out of jail.

The request was unusual. I knew it was a trick. After all, the initiative for making bond is up to the jailed person. And I had made no such request.

But the police and officials were under pressure. Mendenhall was losing money. As a prisoner, I had become a real liability to the town officials.

"I can't make bond," I told them. "I can't do anything without a lawyer."

"Then call him and get him down here to the jail."

I called my lawyer in Jackson. "You stay there," he told me. "Make 'em sweat. Christmas Eve—just before nightfall—make bail then."

The officials kept up their efforts to hurry me out of jail. Of course, the quickest way, dropping charges, was out of the question as they saw it. So they sent up some blacks to urge me to come out—blacks they thought might be willing to forget injustice in the name of "cooperation." But as each one came up I would convince them of what we were doing. All understood, except for one or two who were so sold-out to the system that they couldn't think for themselves anyway.

That evening, Christmas Eve, after the stores were closed, Doug and I announced we would make bail and come out. Christmas Day, everybody tried to pretend it was like other Christmases. But we knew a new road had been taken.

If you talked to black community leaders in most areas like ours and asked them what aggravated the white power structure the most, likely they'd have answered, "There ain't nothin' that makes 'em madder than someone else takin' control of their niggers. And a black man who does that is the worst nigger in the world."

Control is the name of the game. So you can see where that left me. No matter how modest the homes or businesses we wanted to own for ourselves, or how willing we were to cooperate on a normal human basis, just our wanting to own them and run them frightened the whites. And I was the one who was doing the frightening. For the whites could no longer control the black community in the manner to which they had become accustomed, as long as the charges against me stayed unsettled.

But the facts of our arrest did stay unsettled. And the charges remained. So the boycott—our selective buying campaign—continued. And it grew, including more and more blacks from Mendenhall and other nearby towns.

A carefully thought-out list of demands was presented by the black community. It started with the definite problems of the current crisis: dropping all charges against Perkins, Huemmer and Roy Berry, the young man arrested and beaten for presumably making those phone calls.

Then it went on to a fresh statement of American rights for which the black community had been struggling for years. Among them:

"We demand that police obey the U.S. Constitution and Supreme Court orders. Persons must be legally arrested, advised of their rights, rights to remain silent, rights to immediate bail, rights to phone calls, attorney, clean and healthy containment.

"Police, sheriffs, Highway Patrol must have sworn warrant of arrest for any person, or the search of any house, or car.

"We demand that streets in the black community be paved."

Although mishandling by law enforcement officers was an ever-present fear, many of the most crucial points of friction lay in the area of employment and the simple chance to earn a living. There were no blacks in municipal government in key offices such as the welfare office, the jails, the school board, the draft board, the city police and government offices or as court reporters. These were called for in the list of demands.

And in the business community, though they were 31 percent of Simpson County's population, blacks were excluded from most businesses. So 30 percent of employment was demanded. Adherence to the minimum wage was also called for, with special reference to those who worked as maids.

We also called for desegregation of all public facilities, including the schools. (Schools were actually desegregated under court order the following year.)

The whites refused all attempts to discuss our list of demands.

Overall, these senseless arrests, and the absolute refusal to admit any impropriety or mistaken judgment in the handling of the whole affair, had opened a floodgate of emotion in the black community. But through it all, there was nothing illegal or violent in either the list of demands or the method of dramatizing them. All activities in the black community were conducted according to plans; there was no random violence or call for any method that would step outside the boundaries of law.

We were only demanding those rights that were supposedly ours under the Constitution and the present American system. There was no talk of a "new order"; it was only a call to live by the ideals that whites themselves claimed as their heritage.

The boycott continued through January and February. Each Saturday during that time, the leaders of the black community got a parade permit for a march that began at the Voice of Calvary in the black section of town, continued up across the railroad tracks onto Main Street, circled the courthouse and returned.

Do right, white man, do right. Do right, white man, do right.

To the rhythmic chant of "Do right, white man, do right," Nathan Rubin, Curry Brown, Jesse Newsome, Vera Mae and I led the marches, walking in front of the lines. Yes, we were afraid, facing Highway Patrolmen and sheriffs armed with shotguns, gas masks and billy clubs. At the same time, God gave us a bravery that we didn't normally have. We were doing what we had to do, and we knew God was with us.

The most terrible thing about the situation in the South was that so many of the folks who were either violently racist or who participated in discrimination and enslavement through unfair and unlawful business practices called themselves Christians. The question on my mind and on the minds of most black people to whom we preached was whether or not Christianity was a stronger force than racism. In walking the streets, we ourselves were in the role of exhorting our white fellow Christians to repentance and good works.

Far from losing momentum, the weekly parade drew more and more participants each time. College students from Jackson and nearby Tougaloo College joined in, adding momentum to the VOC campaign against oppression. Some Saturdays, as many as 200 chanting young blacks, moving in lines, snaked up and down Main Street.

Do right, white man, do right. Do right, white man, do right.

The black mood those days was one of triumph and excitement. The public assertion of independence proved intoxicating. But the white mood remained one of angry, resentful resistance.

Some blacks lost their jobs. Others had fire insurance policies on their homes cancelled. But the boycott went on.

There was still no move to negotiate in good faith with black leaders selected by the black community or to admit to the botched-up handling of "the Perkins arrest." There were, of course, some contacts with a few blacks selected by the white community as "responsive."

The white town leaders, already wary of what one poorly handled arrest had led to, were beginning to run out of ideas. Or at least any ideas that suited their tastes. So they resorted to the time-honored tradition of divide and conquer.

In hopes of splintering the black community, they reportedly bought off one black minister—then-president of the local NAACP—with $2,000 to oppose the boycott. And he tried to get the boycott called off, but that was impossible by now. He should have known better, even though it had seemed plausible enough to the town's whites, who were observing neither the depth of feeling nor—more important still—the real lines of leadership in the black community.

Meanwhile, other black leaders decided an appropriate reaction to this ploy was necessary. So, for one of their Saturday marches, they invited Dr. Aaron Henry, the highly respected president of the state NAACP, to come to Mendenhall and make a speech. And since Dr. Henry was to lead the march that day, the local NAACP president was asked to introduce the special guest. He agreed and he did.

Dr. Henry made his speech and, without a break at the close, announced that he himself would lead the weekly march uptown. He then linked arms with our local chapter president and began the march.

Caught with blacks he didn't dare alienate—at least in such a public situation—and paralyzed into inaction, our local anti-boycott leader went along numbly with Dr. Henry and with 200 or 300 people following. Up across the tracks we went and into Main Street. White folks, including known Klan members, were standing out on the street watching. And they saw the black "leader," on whom they had spent so much and on whom they had counted to scuttle the boycott, leading the parade himself.

For some strange reason, this minister could never be persuaded to join any further marches. He was seen, at times, talking to individual blacks, trying to persuade them to disassociate themselves from the boycott, but the news of his relationship with the white businessmen put a crimp in his effectiveness.

Boycott leaders organized car pools for buying trips to Jackson. As a result of that, some blacks never really went back to buying in local stores, even after the boycott. It wasn't a continuation of the boycott, but the result of their discovering the wider variety and better prices in the larger city. So they made only occasional local purchases. The boycott thus pushed forward the opening date of a co-op that had been in the works for some time, the Simpson County Co-op Store, owned and operated by local blacks.

No action was taken against any black leaders or members of the community during the boycott itself. But we were all under surveillance by the sheriff's police and by the state Highway Patrol. Cameramen photographed the people in the marches.[1] Observers kept records of every move we made.

Photos for *what*? Records for what?

We wondered.

And we soon found out.

Ambush!

On Saturday, February 7, 1970, Doug and I drove to Tougaloo College near Jackson and picked up a group of their students. The Tougaloo folks supported us all the way in the Mendenhall boycott. And like other Saturdays, they planned to join in our march later that day.

Highway 49 is the main road in and out of Mendenhall. But in town, Highway 13 is the main road in and out of Mendenhall's black section. And the police had set up roadblocks and drivers license checkpoints on Highway 49, Highway 13 and all other roads in and out of Mendenhall.

So both going to Tougaloo and coming back to Voice of Calvary, we had to pass through this control point manned by the police. We were being monitored.[1] But we already knew that. We got monitored every Saturday.

Back in Mendenhall, we rallied with the other demonstrators at our new co-op store. We talked about our selective buying campaign and planned last-minute details of the march. Then when everybody was ready, we took up our signs, formed our parade and headed for the center of town, 100 to 150 strong.

Again, we marched past the roadblock and through the checkpoint. Again, the long lines of our demonstrators flowed up and down Main Street. And once again, their chanting filled the air.

Do right, white man, do right. Do right, white man, do right.

We demonstrated in town for about 45 minutes. While we marched, white bystanders watched and heckled us. State officials watched and took pictures. And all along Main Street—like they did before—sheriffs deputies and Highway Patrolmen with gas masks watched and held weapons at the ready. "Among the official observers was Jonathan Edwards III, the son of the sheriff of neighboring Rankin County, and Inspector Lloyd Jones of the Mississippi Highway Patrol."[2]

After the march through town, we came back to VOC and held a late-afternoon meeting in our church.

Then 19 of the Tougaloo students got into a Dodge van driven by Doug Huemmer for the ride back to Jackson. The rest of the college students piled into VOC's Volkswagen van, driven by Louise Fox. The two vans—with Doug leading and Louise following—left Mendenhall up Highway 49, traveling northwest out of town.

One of the student passengers in Doug's van later testified in court "that the group was followed from Simpson County (Mendenhall) by a Mississippi Highway Patrol car."[3]

Even so, the kids were in high spirits. They clapped their hands and sang freedom songs. They joked about the state officials with their zoom lens cameras snapping pictures of the marchers. They even laughed about the police standing guard with nightsticks and shotguns along the route. In exuberance, one of them again began the chant.

Do right, white man, do right. Do right, white man, do right.

About 6:30 P.M., with the sun just going down, the two vans rolled across the line separating Simpson County from Rankin County. Immediately, near the town of Plain, a Highway Patrol car cut in between the VW van in the rear and Doug's van in front. The patrol car's blue lights signaled Doug to pull over and stop. Right away Doug smelled trouble.

For a routine violation, the driver would be ticketed and sent on. But Doug sensed this was not a "routine" situation. They were away from the community now, out of their home county—the authorities' first real chance to "git those niggers." There just might be complications.

Quick-like, Doug waved to Louise and the folks in the other van to keep on going. He figured they might need to call me. But Louise pulled off the highway and stopped anyway to see what was going to happen.

And here is exactly what did happen that night on Highway 49 and later at the Rankin County Jail in Brandon. I tell part of the story myself. But some of it is best told straight from the official records of the court trial that came later.

Doug pulled the Dodge van onto the hard, red clay shoulder of the road and parked. The patrol car parked behind Doug. A patrolman got out and walked up to the van.

His name? Patrolman Douglas O. Baldwin.

Douglas O. Baldwin, called by the appellants as an adverse witness, was the sole arresting officer. Baldwin is a Patrolman with the Mississippi State Highway Patrol. He testified that he was not in Mendenhall on the day of the law arrests. Prior to the arrests he knew nothing of the identity of the parties.[4]

Yet this was the same Highway Patrolman Douglas O. Baldwin "who had previously been assigned to cover one or two of the Mendenhall marches and who was familiar with the civil rights activities going on there."[5]

Anyway, Baldwin ordered Doug to get out of the van, produce his driver's license and get into the patrol car.

Doug obeyed.

Baldwin later claimed "he had followed the van for four or five miles before stopping it."[6] But why did he stop it? What reason did he have?

> When I came from supper that night I got behind two vans. One was a Dodge van, and the front van was weaving in and out all over the road and I got in between them. The front van was making about 45 or 50 miles an hour, and a car was passing us, we were in a four lane, we were in the outside lane. And this car passed us on the inside lane and he liked [sic] to have hit the car and I stopped him [Huemmer] and got him out, and I didn't know he wasn't the only one in the truck.[7]

Doug and the patrolman sat in the car. And, as Doug himself later testified, Baldwin said to him:

> You almost hit a pickup, and I replied I don't know what you mean because I've been in that same lane for miles. Then he looked up and saw some of the Tougaloo students looking out of the rear windows of the truck at the car, he was about one car's length from the back of the truck, and then he asked me are you some of the demonstrators from Mendenhall and I said yeah and then he just sorta smiled and said, well, we're not going to take any more of this . . . anymore, and we're not going to take any more of this civil rights stuff, and I just didn't say anything and he picked up his microphone and called other units and said I've got a couple of niggers and whites, they are armed, come on down and help me clean them all out tonight, so with that there were a few responses on the radio so then I asked him if I was under

arrest or what was going on and he just didn't say anything else after that, and then he told me to shut up and
if I didn't shut up he was going to shoot me in the head.[8]

Doug shut up.

During the conversation between Baldwin and Huemmer
two students got out of the van to stretch their legs but
were ordered by the officer to get back into the vehicle.
They did. A few minutes later, in response to the radio
request, between four and six Mississippi Highway Patrol
cars arrived at the scene. With pistols drawn the patrolmen ordered all of the students to get out of the van.[9]

It was an eerie sight, what with those blue lights flashing in
the night mist and all those radios crackling and buzzing. The
patrolmen lined the 19 students up against the van, spread their
legs and frisked them. All the time they searched the kids, they
cussed them and damned them as "agitators."

Then a student spoke up and said that one of their group
"was not going to be arrested unless all of them were."[10] He got
his wish. Patrolman Baldwin placed them all under arrest, had
them handcuffed and transported the whole lot to the Rankin
County Jail in Brandon, just a few miles east of Jackson.[11]

Doug "was taken in a separate car and beaten enroute and
after arrival at the jail by Officer Frank Thames of the Highway
Patrol."[12] He later reported:

After the students were handcuffed and taken off, I was
pulled out of the car and handcuffed by Officer Thames,
and one or two of the other officers were going to put me
in another patrol car with some of the other students and

Officer Thames said, no I want him for myself and went and put me in the back seat of Officer Baldwin's patrol car; then Officer Thames got in the passenger side of Officer Baldwin's car with Officer Baldwin driving the car and we left then for the jail, and I was still handcuffed, and then he turned around and said I told you last summer if you didn't get out of this civil rights stuff I was going to take care of you, and then he turned around and slapped me a few times in the face, and then he told me to turn around so he could take the handcuffs off. He took the handcuffs off of my right hand and it was still on my left hand and he pulled my hand down until my hand went down on the front seat and then he continued to slap or hit me and as we would pass another car or another truck on the highway he would stop, and then as we would go by the car or truck he would start again. Then he was hitting me in my face with his fist then he took the other handcuff off and stored it someplace and then he took me by my hair and twisted me so that my neck was kinda bent and punched me in my groin, my stomach and my face and my neck and then pushed me over toward Officer Baldwin who hit me a couple of times.[13]

All during this he was saying he had warned me about civil rights stuff, that he didn't give a damn about civil rights stuff, that I was a damn Cuban, and called me a . . . Moscow man, and all sort of other profanity, and then when we got to the jail we stopped in an alley, it's an alley between the jail and the parking lot and I stayed in the back seat for about thirty or forty minutes and I could see from the window up in the jail where I guess they were processing other students and during the time they kept me in the car out in the alley he would contin-

ue to come every two or three minutes and open the door
and kick me or slap me and he kept worrying me with
saying, I want to kill you tonight that's what I wanted,
that he wasn't going to kill me but he was going to teach
me a lesson and this lasted for about 30 minutes.[14]

This was going on outside the jail. But inside the Brandon
Jail, all the Tougaloo College students were being booked on
charges ranging from "reckless driving" to "carrying a concealed
deadly brick." Al Todd, one of the students involved, said later,
"They took us to the Brandon Jail and booked us. They called us
names and beat us with blackjacks and billy clubs and they
kicked and stomped us."

Meanwhile, as soon as the Highway Patrolmen drove away
with Doug and the students, Louise Fox got to a phone in Plain,
Mississippi, and called us in Mendenhall. We could hear fear in
her voice. She was crying. "The people in Doug's van have been
locked up in Brandon," she told us.

Brandon! We knew all about Brandon. Sheriff Jonathan
Edwards there had beaten blacks just for registering to vote.[15]
Compared to Brandon, Mendenhall was a liberated place!

As soon as I heard what happened from Louise, I told her to
take the rest of the students on to Tougaloo College. Then I got
hold of Rev. Curry Brown and Joe Paul Buckley. We set out for
Brandon and the Rankin County Jail to post bail for Doug and
his group.

Doug—and the kids with him—had run into an ambush out
there on Highway 49. Yet the same police who arrested them let
Louise and her van load of passengers go free. Why? Because
they knew she would call us and tell us to come? Was there
another ambush out there on that highway—waiting for us?

We had to go.

Rev. Brown and I drove up Highway 49. It was a 45-minute drive, but we hardly spoke during the trip. A lot was going on in my mind just then. In a way, it was like the replay of a bad dream.

Highway 49. Twenty-four years before I had raced along this same road, between these same fields and farms. Someone else had been driving that night, too—the night my brother Clyde was killed.

But Curry, Joe Paul and I never made bond for the students that night in Brandon. When we got to the courthouse and jail, a Highway Patrolman outside showed us where to park. We got out of the car and stood beside it talking for a couple minutes. We had met no ambush on Highway 49.

"We'd like to see the sheriff," we told the patrolman.

"Okay," he said. "You stay here, and I'll go tell him you're here."

But then instead of the sheriff coming to see us, about a dozen Highway Patrolmen came out of the building, searched us and arrested us. "Among the arresting officers was Inspector Lloyd Jones of the Highway Patrol, who earlier in the day had participated in the surveillance activities at Mendenhall."[16]

"Goon" Jones and I had met again!

So it was an ambush after all! Only here at the jail-house, instead of out on Highway 49! They'd set this up. And we'd fallen right into their trap. What innocent fools we were!

The bad dream of Highway 49 became a nightmare. Even before they got us into the building, the police started beating us. Curry caught it bad right away from Officer Thames while he was being taken into the jail. Curry later reported at the trial:

Officer Thames took me up the driveway, and as he was taking me and we started up the driveway he started kicking me in the back, he kicked me in the kidney and slapped me back of my head and I don't know if he was hitting me with his hand or hitting me with something but he did this all the way up to the jail door and then he shoved me inside.[17]

Inside the jailhouse, the nightmare just got worse. At least five deputy sheriffs and seven to twelve Highway Patrolmen went to work on us. Sheriff Edwards joined in.[18]

When I got to the jail and saw the people in the jail, of course I was horrified as to why we were arrested and when I got in the jail Sheriff Jonathan Edwards came over to me right away and said, this is the smart nigger, and this is a new ballgame, *you're not in Simpson County now, you are in Brandon*, and we began, and uh, he began to beat me, and from that time on they continued beating me, I was just beat to the floor and just punched and just really beaten.[19]

Manorris Odom, one of the Tougaloo students present, said he saw Sheriff Edwards beat me so hard his "shirt tail came out."[20] During the beatings, I tried to cover my head with my arms, but they just beat me anyway till I was lying on the floor. Even then they just kept on beating and stomping me, kicking me in the head, in the ribs, in the groin. I rolled up in a ball to protect myself as best I could.

The beatings just went on and on. Would the agony never end?

The police had moonshine whiskey in the jail with them that night, "although the sheriff did strenuously deny that any of his men had been drinking or were drunk during the hours in question."[21] But whatever the beverage was—in between beating us—

several deputies sipped it steadily from mysterious-smelling paper cups. Then—in between the sips—they went back to work on us, fast and mad. And then faster and madder.

The moonshine seemed to serve many purposes. Some time during the night, the sheriffs deputies shaved the heads of both Curry and Doug. Then Sheriff Edwards "personally poured moonshine whiskey on Huemmer's head."[22]

Because I was unconscious a lot of the time, I don't remember much about the others. In fact, I don't remember a whole lot about me, except that there was blood all over. And a lot of it was mine.

I know that some of the students were beaten. And Doug, too. Doug doesn't remember a whole lot either because he was unconscious a good deal of the time himself. But he saw and remembered enough to testify later:

Sheriff Edwards and Sheriff Edwards' son and two Highway Patrolmen that I don't know the names of and Officer Thames had a leather blackjack thing and they began beating on Reverend Brown, Reverend Perkins, David Nall and myself and one of the other students, and they beat Reverend Brown down to the floor and then Reverend Perkins was dragged over on the other side and beaten down by about five other officers. I could hear him being beaten and then I was knocked out and when I came to I heard them ordering Reverend Perkins to mop up the blood that was on the floor. By this time David Nall was bleeding all over the floor and Reverend Perkins was lying sorta stunned on the floor and they kicked him until he got up . . . then Sheriff Edwards, Sheriff Edwards' son, and two or three patrol officers would walk by every two or three minutes and kick or hit Reverend Perkins with one of their blackjacks or their feet.[23]

That mopping-up business Doug told about was no sudden fit of tidiness on the part of the police. Sometime in the middle of all that mayhem, word came over the radio that the FBI might be coming. Well, it wouldn't do to have blood all over the floor while entertaining the FBI. So they ordered me to take a mop and start cleaning up.

I did my best, but I was so weak and wobbly and in so much pain. Blood was still pouring from my head, and it didn't help a whole lot that some of the police kept on beating me while I tried to mop up my own blood. Then they had me go into a back room and wash up nice and clean for our federal visitors.

But no FBI. They never came.

The false report angered the patrolmen even more than before. They cursed me and began beating me again, making up for the time they lost. But I guess the FBI threat made them remember at least some legal niceties. They took me into another room, photographed me and started taking my fingerprints.

But even then they couldn't leave me alone. While they were taking my prints, one officer took a pistol, put it to my head and pulled the trigger. Then another officer—a bigger one—beat me unconscious again.

After I came to this time, they decided they wanted a performance. They had found a copy of the printed demands of the black community of Mendenhall. And not content with just a crude beating, they ordered me to read the demands aloud as entertainment for the party.

I could hardly see to read, and I was having real trouble breathing. Besides, my throat was all banged up and swollen. So I couldn't read loud enough to suit them.

"Nigger, read louder!" they'd shout.

Or, in mock conversation with each other, "Y'know, I can't stand a nigger who can't read loud."

How long all this went on, and who did what, I don't even know. I do know it got worse as the night wore on.

[When] they started torturing us, it was horrifying, I couldn't even imagine that this was happening, one of the officers took a fork that was bent down and he brought that fork up to me and he said, have you seen this, and he took that fork and put that fork into my nose, then he took that fork and pushed it down my throat, and then they took me over there and beat me to the ground, and Officer Thames, he was doing most of the talking, and then they beat me to the floor and Mr. Lloyd Jones was sitting down on the front . . . and he got up and stomped me and by this time I was almost out.[24]

They were like savages—like some horror out of the night. And I can't forget their faces, so twisted with hate. It was like looking at white-faced demons. Hate did that to them.

But you know, I couldn't hate back. When I saw what hate had done to them, I couldn't hate back. I could only pity them. I didn't ever want hate to do to me what it had already done to those men.

At long last, the thud, thud, thud of those awful beatings stopped. Then they took me upstairs and put me into the hands of two jailers who hadn't been in on the other beating. I guess they wanted to get their licks in too, because they started beating me again on the way to the cell. But by this time, my head and body had become so numb that I could feel their weight but they inflicted no pain. I remember only vaguely some of the Tougaloo students helping me to a bed. But things seemed strangely out of balance. I felt like the bed kept turning up while I lay there.

The rest of the night pain flooded back and forth through my body. Drifting in and out of consciousness. Something cool on my head. A wet cloth placed there carefully by one of the students. And again something cool. A student's shirt soaked in cold water. They cared for me through the rest of the night.

It was God's providence that Vera Mae had not gone with us to Brandon. She could have done nothing to help and stood a good chance of ending up in jail herself.

Somebody—I think it was Louise Fox again—called Vera Mae and told her we three had been locked up. Vera Mae called Anna Buckley, Joe Paul's wife, and said, "Let's get together and try to get Brother Curry, Brother John and Brother Joe Paul out of jail."

But how to get to Brandon? Louise had the van and had stayed up at Tougaloo College with the kids there. And she wasn't about to come driving down Highway 49 again that night after seeing Doug arrested. Herbert—one of the guys that worked with us—was gone with the station wagon. And our little red VW and the other van were already in Brandon. So they agreed to wait till morning.

Vera Mae went to bed hurting real bad. She knew nothing of what had happened in Brandon, but not knowing was hard, too. So she couldn't sleep. She just lay there wondering and feeling helpless.

Along about one in the morning, she got a phone call. A man's voice asked, "Have they hung them yet?"

"Hung who?" Vera Mae spluttered. "And who's this calling?"

"This is Sted Hayes."

"This is not Sted Hayes's voice. Who is this?" The caller hung up, leaving Vera Mae to wonder who it was. All she knew was the voice was white.

In the morning, Vera Mae found someone with a car and got to Brandon about nine o'clock. There's this real broad street in front of the jailhouse. And a lawn around it with an iron fence around that. There's no way to describe to others what it feels like for a black person to walk in a place like that.

That morning when Vera Mae and the others arrived, a lot of white men were standing and sitting around the jailhouse. Folks we'd call Klan types. Just hanging around real casual-like, but with sharp alert faces, seeing everything, missing nothing. Some were chewing and spitting tobacco. On their faces was that kind of half-smile that's not really a smile.

Vera Mae, Mrs. Buckley, Larry Buckley, Mrs. Stanfield and the others started up to the jailhouse. From one of the upper windows in the jail section, Joe Paul had been watching. He saw them coming.

"Go back!" he yelled. "Go back! Don't let Larry and those other boys in here. The sheriff said he'd shoot them!"

I knew they'd be scared. They had to be. Anybody with sense would be scared. But they had to do something. They went on in to the jailhouse.

Sheriff Edwards met them. "Ain't nobody going in but the mothers and wives. So all you others go back!"

Mrs. Buckley said, "I'm Joe Paul's wife."

"My son's in there," said Mrs. Stanfield.

"And I'm Mrs. Perkins," Vera Mae told the sheriff.

The officers led me to the room where Vera Mae was waiting. I was so weak and in so much pain, I couldn't stand. They had to give me a chair to sit in. Vera Mae stood there with a policeman only inches behind her. We could have no privacy.

Whatever Vera Mae was feeling and thinking, she hid it real good. I knew I looked horrible. Sores and blood and all. And my eyes bulging right out of my head. In the background, the younger students were yelling. There was no way she couldn't hear them.

I sat there holding my head in agony. And Vera Mae sort of made her arms and shoulders real big, as she reached down and around me. So The Man couldn't hear.

She kept saying, "What happened to you, what happened to you?" She whispered low and painful.

"Vera Mae," I said, "get me out of here. Get me out of here because they gonna kill me first." I couldn't say much more than that.

"Toop, honey, let me see what I can do."

Only later did Vera Mae learn from some of the Tougaloo students who had nursed me through the night that they were sure for a while I was dead—or about to die.

But right then—with 23 of us still behind bars—it was time to work. Mr. Nathan Rubin, Civic League president of Simpson County, started riding all over Rankin County, looking for blacks with property—blacks with property willing to post it as bond. Mr. Rubin, who ran a stump-hauling business himself, had relatives in Rankin County and a lot of contacts there. Men like J. D. Hill, John Adam, Henry Griffin and M. J. Mangum willingly put up their property—despite the taunts of the officer at the desk, who warned them they would lose everything. Other friends offered to help, too, but none of them owned enough property to cover the bonds. All of them were turned away.

Then at last an old lady—and a friend, Alfoncia Hill—who owned enough property to cover my bond, walked bravely into Sheriff Edwards's office, signed the bond and walked out. I was released about three o'clock that Sunday afternoon.

I'll never forget the gigantic dimensions of these noble tributes. But there still wasn't enough bond for all. We needed $5,000 bond alone just for Curry. So even with his terrible head injuries, Curry had to spend all that Sunday night in jail. And the officers there taunted him throughout the night. They told him all his friends had deserted him. That nobody was coming back for him.

Finally, about 5:00 P.M. on Monday, we got Curry Brown out of jail. He was the last one out. But now he too could go home.

Mr. Luvell Purvis lived not too far from the Brandon jail. He not only helped raise our bail, but he also opened up his house as a refuge for the released prisoners as we gradually bailed everybody out. His home became a sanctuary like the home of John Mark's mother where they joyfully welcomed Peter after he was released from prison.

Mr. Purvis had once been a barber. Now carefully, gently, he trimmed the hair away from my wounds. In every way, this quiet, dignified man did all he could to ease the anguish each of us had suffered.

I was still there at Mr. Mangum's when Curry, the last one to be bailed, was brought into the house. This beloved brother of mine. He had probably suffered more than any of us. For a moment, we could only look at each other. Then we just wrapped our arms around each other and hugged and cried.

Dear God, the nightmare was over.

And we were free!

Beyond Brandon

For a long time after Brandon, our hearts and bodies were sore.
And both were slow in healing. I imagine the scars will always be
there.

We were all badly wounded and terribly bruised. And a lot of
us had lost blood. One of the students had got his teeth knocked
out. Curry had deep cuts in the back of his head. And I had injuries
all over my body. A week after Brandon, the knot of blood on my
head was so big and soft, the doctor had to draw out almost a cup
of fluid to get it to go down.

Our injuries were treated by Dr. Robert Smith, a good friend
and a real dedicated black physician. I guess we kept him kinda
busy for a while. As a black professional, Dr. Smith could have set
up shop in lots of other places where the work was easier and the
money bigger. But he stayed and set up practice here in Mississippi.

So he has had his finger on the pulse of the racial conflict. In
fact, he participated in marches in Jackson and around the state.
He totally supported the movement.

I remember one conversation Dr. Smith shared with me. It
was after attending a medical conference at a local hotel with a
white colleague who was trying to spell out to him how well
things had progressed in black-white relations. The white doctor pointed out that they were now able to attend the same
medical conventions, eat together at the same restaurants and,

in general, have more contact than in previous years.

"And who knows," the white doctor added as the ultimate in optimism, "maybe not too long from now you will even be able to attend our church."

The doctor made the statement straight forward. No irony intended. It obviously never entered that white churchman's mind that progress in black-white relations should begin—not end—in the church. Nor did he seem aware that many of the most systematic haters are ministers and Sunday School teachers. In fact, most of the outstanding killings and murderings of blacks in the South have had white ministers involved in them. This was true even of the killing and secret burying of the three civil rights workers in Philadelphia, Mississippi, in 1964.

One Sunday, Curry and Doug went to a white Baptist church in Mendenhall. And there they joined with the rest of the congregation in the singing of the "Doxology."

Praise God, from whom all blessings flow—

Clomp, clomp, clomp! Over the sound of the music came the thud of heavy feet stomping up the aisle. It was the chief of police.

Praise Him, all creatures here below—

The chief stopped by Curry and Doug's pew. Even before he spoke, his face showed clearly what he felt.

"You weren't invited here. The congregation, the minister and I don't want you here. Get out!"

Praise Him above, ye heavenly host—

They got out!

Praise Father, Son and Holy Ghost.

At Brandon, the white community had made it clear that it would go to any length—to the brink of murder—to prevent blacks from having their rights. I began to see then that the net effect of black agitation had been a hardening of white attitudes, not the softening I had hoped for.

And there were other reminders as well as to where we stood.

A few days after Brandon, Curry sent someone to pick up his van at the garage where the police had towed it. But the attendant said he had orders from the sheriff to let no one but the owner pick it up. Also, he was supposed to call the sheriff so the sheriff could come before the vehicle was released.

That seemed odd to Curry, but later on he went down to the garage himself. A white civil rights worker went with him. The attendant called the sheriffs office and learned the sheriff was tied up in court. So contrary to the sheriffs orders and without the sheriff being there, he let the vehicle go.

The next day Curry went out to his van to get some tools and a change of work clothes, so he could do some carpentry work. A few minutes later he came into the house where Vera Mae was working, his hand shaking like a leaf. And in his hand, he held a deadly sharp straight razor.

He had found the razor in one of his boots. But it wasn't his. He had never seen it before. Someone had placed it there.

"Sister," he said to Vera Mae, "now I know why they didn't let Herbert pick up this van the other day. They were going to come, follow me and arrest me on the road. Then they'd search the van and find this 'concealed weapon.' Sister, they were sure 'nuff going to kill me."

And, in the following weeks, just as another reminder, the local patrolman who cruised by VOC would hold up his shotgun and wave it at Curry whenever Curry was outside working.

Just a reminder.

After Brandon, I got to wondering more about white folks. After all, they're people, too. Human beings just like us. And all of us made in the image of God, even though the image has gotten pretty bent and cracked at times.

You know, people—being people—don't do anything without some sort of reason. It may not be a very good reason. And I may think it is a pretty poor reason. But I figure there has to be a reason of some sort.

So I wondered.

Take Brandon, for instance. That whole Brandon mess was something you wouldn't even dream people could do to each other. But they did. Why? For what reason?

At first, the reasons weren't very clear. But after I was beaten by white policemen, I began to see things a little more clearly. I was able to see the needs of white people and what racism was doing to them. You see, I had gotten set to the fact that the sickness of racism had affected the black community in a way that kept them from functioning as a healthy community. A lot of our people were sick—affected by generations of slavery, oppression and exploitation—psychologically destroyed. But I had never thought much before about how all that had affected whites—how *they* had been affected by racism, by attitudes of racial superiority, by unjust lifestyles and behavior.

Now I wondered a lot.

You see, there was nothing special about the Brandon beatings. There have been plenty more like them. And I mean beatings like this by police officers and Highway Patrol, not just by mobs. But why? For what reason?

I saw an article in *Time* magazine on the Mississippi Highway Patrol that included a discussion of my case. That article was sort of asking why, too. It said, "It is unfair to put all the blame on the patrol for its poor performance in racial situations, for the state's present leaders would have it no other way. To them, the force is an admirable efficient defender of Mississippi's traditional way of life."[1]

The article also quoted a legal observer as saying, "Highway patrol members are much like policemen everywhere. They do what is expected of them or tolerated by their superiors—nothing more or less."

So official sanction was one of the reasons.[2] And a "see no evil" acquiescence by the public—including Christians—was another. Yes, that also made a contribution.

I wouldn't have expected most good Americans of that day to believe that such things—like what happened to us at Brandon—still happened in this country. I wouldn't expect them to believe how the police and the Highway Patrol had that thing planned and how those people acted.

Whites would probably have said, "It's almost too much to believe. Who would be so stupid as to beat someone like that in jail?"

And most white Christians would not have wanted to believe this either. Instead, they would have closed their eyes to it. Why? Because if a white person minded his own business, he went up the ladder. He didn't get in trouble. So he figured that a black guy who got in trouble just wasn't obeying the law. (Thirty years later, too many still think this way.)

But, "it ain't necessarily so."

And that's why I wonder sometimes.

And what of the law officers themselves? I wonder about them, too. You can't just label their actions "sin" and forget it. They have their own set of reasons. But what are they?

I began looking at the Highway Patrol. Really looking. And I began to see what kind of person becomes a guard or patrolman in Mississippi. It's the kind of person who's just got to carry a gun, wear a uniform and all.

You see, there is a kind of white person who has nothing going for him in life except his whiteness and racism. And too often this kind of person goes out and joins the police force or the Highway Patrol. It gives him a chance to make himself feel important by brutalizing a black.

Everybody needs to feel important—*because he or she is*. But brutality is something like dope. Some people have to have it to confirm themselves. It's a sickness of the racist.

Now, I don't mean every single policeman is like this, but the occupation does lure many of this type. It attracts this kind of person to the uniform, and I don't see any effective effort to keep such types out.

Say you're black and you're stopped by a white highway patrolman. If the officer happens to be one of those I'm referring to, he'll ask you questions. But not questions that require sentences for answers. He doesn't really want to talk with you. So his questions are just ones you can answer with "yes, sir" or "no, sir." And after you've answered all his questions, he may make you repeat the answers all over again. It confirms him as someone with authority.

But I still wonder.

Some people have a little more in their favor than their whiteness and racism. These are people who have standing in their community, like a respected insurance man. For these folks, racism takes the form of paternalism.

This kind of person already has the respect no "po' cracker" is ever going to get. But it still isn't enough. So where do such folks get that additional respect they think they need in order to have self-respect? Out of black folks.

This form of racism is more funny than brutal. Go to any small town or county seat and look around the courthouse or stores where white folks and black folks sit around on benches. On a hot day, some white person who has gathered a little extra money might walk up to where some black man is sitting and say, "Would you like to have a drink on me, Bill?"

And Bill will say, "Yes, sir, Mister Smith."

So they will go into the store, and the white man will say, real casual like, "Get what you want, Bill," and maybe he'll include two or three other blacks as well.

So outside, everybody is standing around, sipping their soft drinks, and the blacks will be saying a few polite, kind words about Mr. Smith. And the "Mister Smith" types *have to* have that. Innocent as it all looks, it is people with that same kind of need that join the police force or become guards, even sometimes moving out of the South to some big city to do it. And when you put that kind of mentality up against black folks who are finally trying to find their own identity—well, you've got a real problem.

The point is, against that kind of mentality, blacks don't have to be militant to have trouble with the law. No black who is just trying to be human is going to come up with the "right" answers. Any act of his—or even no act at all—can be called "hostility." And in that kind of situation, there is no such thing as the black having a choice of "violence" or "nonviolence."[3]

So that's the problem. And that problem is the kind of thing that white conservative Christians, miles from the situation, miss entirely when they criticize any black efforts or projects aimed toward just being human.

Do you see why I wonder?

Mississippi
Justice

Nine days after the Brandon incident, I was to take my first step down the long legal road of *Perkins v. State of Mississippi*. On February 16, 1970, I would face a nonjury trial before a justice of the peace.[1] On what charge or charges? I did not know. My lawyers did not know.

You see, the nature of the charge lodged against me on December 23, 1969—the night Doug and I were arrested and detained overnight in the Mendenhall jail—had never been known to me. I had never been informed of any particular statute I was supposed to have violated. This made preparing a case a little hard for my lawyers.

With that kind of a situation there seemed little hope of getting a fair hearing locally. Infected with the same sickness of racism that afflicts all of Mississippi, the local courts could be counted on to have only one point of view. So, still weak from the physical battering I had received in Brandon, I prayed more than ever for God's strength, not only for the ability to get through the legal ordeal ahead of me, but to do so as a man who could stand for righteousness without bitterness or vindictiveness.

My lawyers knew we would lose our case in Mendenhall, no matter what the evidence might be. So their strategy was to lay out enough objections to give us some sort of chance for appeal.

On February 16, I went before the justice of the peace. The whole trial was conducted without reference to any statute. The J. P.'s verdict was based only on his finding that I had performed certain alleged actions. But whether or how these actions violated a particular stated law was never discussed. The quick and certain verdict: guilty, with punishment of a $300 fine and three months in county jail.

We appealed. A person who appeals a justice of the peace verdict and asks for a trial by jury is not re-tried. He is given a trial *de novo*—new from the beginning. So less than a month later—on March 16, 1970—my new trial began with Circuit Court Judge Joseph A. McFarland, Jr., presiding.

The courtroom in the Simpson County Courthouse is tall with a horseshoe-shaped balcony. The balcony is seldom used. So seldom, in fact, that only the large central area of the courtroom was given a new white tile ceiling. Over the balcony is the same old ceiling, painted black. But today, for this trial, the balcony was full.

The jury didn't sit in what could be called a jury box, but in a large area to the judge's right, in front of a tall window. Although the original jury list contained names of some blacks, the jury selection was all-white.

My lawyers were all from the Lawyers' Committee for Civil Rights Under Law, an organization formed with representatives from the nation's leading law firms following a meeting with President John Kennedy in 1963. The lawyers were led by a young black woman recently out of law school, Constance Iona Slaughter, and more seasoned practitioners: Lawrence Ross, James Robertson and James Abram.

The lawyers began their groundwork for later appeal with a series of objections, such as objecting to the all-white composition of the jury. So county officials were called on to testify on the methods of drawing up jury lists. One supervisor said, "If I know someone personally and I know he won't make a good juror, I don't put his name down." Aside from eliciting that statement and entering into the record statistics on the percentage of blacks in Simpson County, nothing more could be done about the jury. The judge ruled against all motions by the defense.

Another problem: I still had not been informed of any statute I was supposed to have violated. So now, before Judge McFarland, the defense moved to dismiss the indictment or to continue only after the defendant was informed of a statutory violation in the charge.

This move provoked a bit of wrangling. The District Attorney, W. D. Adams, insisted that he had never been asked by the defense for such a specific piece of information. Defense lawyers retorted that they had indeed asked. But in any case, they shouldn't have had to ask; it was theirs by right.

My lawyers wanted to know how they could prepare our case without knowing how the specific statute was framed that I was charged with violating. Otherwise, we could not show whether or not my conduct fell under its provisions. Finally, the D.A. came up with the necessary information. The state had charged that I, Rev. John M. Perkins, "did willfully and unlawfully contribute to the delinquency of a minor under the age of sixteen years, whose name is Georgia Ann Quinn, willfully and unlawfully inducing and persuading said minor to enter and remain in the Simpson County Jail contrary to the instructions of Jimmy Griffiths, jailer of Simpson County . . ."

Considering the way the evidence was stacked, there seemed little hope of an acquittal or a "not guilty" verdict. In the affidavit sworn to by the jailer, the name "Georgia Ann Quinn" was written in a different hand from the rest of the document. Originally the word "unknown" had been written in and was still legible, though scratched over.

This document was only one link in a chain of Alice-in-Wonderland developments that grew out of a "verdict first then the trial" mentality. Once having decided that I had to have committed a crime, they had to find a specific child whose delinquency I had contributed to. But just sticking the child's name on the document did not get them completely over their difficulty. They still had to show some link between me and the girl's acts. And there was the problem of proving that the jailer who made the charge even knew the girl was there at the time. But Mississippi justice knows how to cope with such problems.

A principal prosecution witness was Jimmy Griffiths, the jailer who signed the original charges. The prosecution version of events required them to establish Griffiths's willingness to release every young person so that their presence in the jail could only be the result of my persuasion. That was the only way I could be guilty of contributing to the delinquency of 11-year-old Georgia Ann Quinn.

But on cross-examination, the deputy's supposed concern for the youngsters in his care showed itself in strange ways. First he admitted he had locked the door on them all. How then, asked the astonished defense attorney, were they supposed to leave?

"Well," Griffiths replied, "we did lock the door behind them, but they were free to leave at any time. We almost begged them to leave."

He further admitted that when they started pounding on the door, he opened a slot from his side to spray in some Mace. Griffiths never really tried to explain these and other curious events of that night; he merely bypassed them to continue his insistence of concern for the young people.

In Mendenhall, as in other small county seats, a deputy often was assigned various duties. Besides acting as jailer, Griffiths also served frequently as a courtroom deputy. The fact that he was a prosecution witness in the present trial did not bother the court officials; he remained in his usual place as a bailiff when not on the witness stand. During one recess, he was observed standing in the jury area and even exchanging words with one of the jurors.

A defense lawyer objected and drew a sharp rebuke from the judge: "You've just come into my courtroom a few minutes, and already you're telling me how to run the thing!"

The defense then asked for consultation in the judge's chambers, out of hearing of the jury. There they moved for a mistrial. The judge, after hearing Griffiths tell his version of the conversation with the juror, ruled it inconsequential and overruled the motion.

Judge McFarland appeared amazed that anyone should object to a situation in which a prosecution witness is also a court bailiff and hangs around the jury area. But he grudgingly agreed to rule that deputies and other law officers stay away from the jury for the rest of the trial.

However, the hearing in the judge's chambers had revealed another interesting point. The content of the conversation with the juror, as reported by Griffiths, clearly showed that there was a personal acquaintance between Griffiths and the juror, yet during the selection of the jury each prospective juror had claimed in court that he had *no* personal acquaintance with the state witness, Griffiths. It would be difficult to pin this down on appeal, however, because of another defense difficulty: no transcript was made of the *voir dire*—the examination of prospective jurors.

Then Georgia Ann Quinn, 11 years old, was called by the prosecution to testify how she came to be part of the group that went up to visit the jail. Although she was called as a prosecution witness, none of the District Attorney's questions succeeded in undermining her assertion that I had made no effort to persuade her to come to the jail or to remain there.

The trial went on for two days—a lot longer than most trials of this kind. The whole business was beginning to get to me.

While I was on the stand, prosecuting attorneys accused me of every kind of vileness. I began to despair. There was no way that I could refute their charges, not in this courtroom before this all-white jury. They were breaking me, and I knew it. Maybe they knew it, too.

Finally the judge gaveled a recess. I made my way back to a water fountain near the courtroom entrance and stood there a moment in abject misery. Then I walked out, alone. Other blacks would have crowded around me, had we been winning the case. But now, people didn't know what to say, didn't want to burden me.

Then a little black woman—I guess she had followed me out—came up to me, face to face with me. She was perhaps 75, with dark skin and a square jaw. She looked right at me, and I felt her blazing eyes—under that huge, floppy hat—bore right through me. In a soft, commanding voice, she said, "Stand up, son!"

That's all, just "Stand up, son!"

God must have sent her; she was just what I needed. I will never forget that face and those three words. Yes, I *could* stand up. I *would* stand up. Because I knew I wasn't standing alone! I wasn't standing just for myself.

I sucked in my stomach. Threw back my shoulders. With new stamina in my heart, I walked back into that courtroom, ready for round two.

The trial went on. My defense lawyers attacked every statement of the charge. In order to be "contributing to the delinquency of a minor," they claimed, you must first have a delinquent minor. That sounded sensible. But there was nothing in Miss Quinn's behavior at any time to establish her delinquency, or even potential delinquency—as delinquency is defined by the statute.

Also, they claimed, you must have behavior by the defendant that could contribute to such delinquency and must establish that said behavior was in fact the motive force behind the minor's acts. All of which the prosecution failed to do.

And, of course, there was the overwhelming evidence that all the disputed events resulted from the jailer's acts, not mine, since all of us would have come and gone peaceably and legally, if we had been allowed to.

But all the defense maneuvering was to no avail. I was found guilty as charged, the jury requiring only a few minutes to reach this decision. For my "arrogance" in appealing the earlier sentence of $300 and three months—pronounced by the justice of the peace—I was now sentenced to pay a fine of $400 and spend four months in county jail.

Our defense attorneys then filed motions of appeal to the state Supreme Court. That meant the preparation of more documents. The appeal was duly considered some months later.

Out of all the defense points for appeal, one was granted as a reversible error: the issue of a state witness also serving as bailiff and conversing with a juror. This, of course, didn't touch on the real question of whether I contributed to the delinquency of a minor. But it did put an extra burden on the lower court: either give me another trial or drop the charges.

In that situation the best that my lawyers could do was a bit of horse trading. They had already filed a suit against the county protesting the all-white jury as being nonrepresentative of the county electorate. So they still held that one card in their favor.

But since there was yet an unresolved charge of disturbing the peace, a bargain was struck. I would plead guilty to that lesser charge and drop my suit against the county. In court, the District Attorney would then make a public statement that it was "not in the best interest of Simpson County" to bring me to trial again on the delinquency charge.

No one won, and no one lost. But justice, Mississippi style, had been served.

Yet what turned out to be only a draw on paper was, in many ways, a real victory for the black community of Mendenhall. Like the boycott, the Mendenhall trial had helped to unify the black community.

And for the first time, our people saw a young black woman lawyer—a Mississippi black woman, at that—stand in Mendenhall's courtroom and argue a major case. That had never happened before in Simpson County.

They also saw a local black go into that courtroom, lose a case and come out without going to jail. So our people saw that losing a case in the local court wasn't the end of the road anymore. They saw us appeal all the way to the Mississippi Supreme Court.

And they saw what the Supreme Court did. When the Supreme Court found how rigged and tricky the administration of justice was on the local level, the Supreme Court sent the case back to the local court and told them to settle it right there. They did. And our people saw that.

So, in a real sense, someone did lose and someone did win. The local court lost the power to intimidate blacks. And local blacks won a great moral victory. The inspiration of that victory still motivates and liberates Mendenhall's black community today.

At the Gates
of Justice

The law was not finished with us yet. Even before the Mendenhall trial began, all of us who were arrested and beaten that brutal night in Brandon had to begin our journey through another legal labyrinth. As a result of the events in Brandon, 23 defendants—the students arrested on Highway 49, several VOC co-workers and myself—were all charged with various crimes.

I was charged with "resisting arrest." Some of the students were also charged with "resisting arrest," although it was never determined what acts constituted the offense or where the acts occurred. Among the several other charges was "carrying a concealed, deadly brick," which had been found in the back of the van. A "deadly" brick—in contrast to any other kind—was never defined.

Five days after the Brandon incident, our lawyers petitioned to have our pending state criminal prosecution removed to the United States District Court. And a date was set for the U.S. District Court to hear our petition for removal.

"Removal" is a term common to many civil rights cases throughout the country. You see, Congress had passed laws protecting all marches, sit-ins, demonstrations and other civil rights activities. This made it certain that when people were arrested for taking part in these activities, they would be tried in federal courts—and not be subject to the more prejudiced local courts.

To get around this, local authorities would arrest civil rights people on charges that seemed "unrelated" to the civil rights activities themselves. Then they'd be tried in state courts. This was the reason the students were arrested in another county. They were trying to nail us without our going to a federal court.

So our big legal struggle was to try to get our case "removed" from state to federal courts.

The first court to hear our case was the District Court. What they did was to narrow down the meaning of removal to such a small definition that it could not even be applied to our case.

Getting beaten in Brandon was dehumanizing. But to see logical and rational minds applied to legalizing the cause of racism was almost too much to take.

Our petition for removal was denied, and we were ordered to stand trial in the state courts.[1] This, to us, meant certain conviction on false charges.

But that order was stayed as our lawyers appealed our petition for removal to the United States Court of Appeals. On January 14, 1972, a three-judge panel heard the appeal. By a two-to-one vote, appeal was denied.

Forming the majority on the court were Judge Clark and Judge James P. Coleman. Coleman was a former state Attorney General and a former governor of the state of Mississippi. The dissenting vote was cast by the chief judge of the 15-member bench of the U.S. Court of Appeals, Judge John R. Brown.

The opinion against us written by the majority covers only 11 pages in the court records. But Judge Brown's dissent goes well over 100 pages and is, in itself, a detailed indictment of a legal system gone sour. And he registered his stinging dissent on several grounds.

First, as to the facts of the case: There was no evidence at all for the charges against us, so there was slim ground for any reasoning used by the state to deny removal. As to the charges against us, Judge Brown declared:

> The complexities we face are not factual ones. We need not resolve credibility choices or conflicting inferences to determine what happened to these petitioners. No matter whose version is accepted the record is replete with uncontested evidence of patently frivolous arrests for nonexistent offenses, threatened and actual physical violence, and almost unbelievably humiliating and degrading treatment—including the indignity of shaving the prisoners' heads and pouring moonshine whiskey on one of them—that far surpasses the official brutality we have only recently condemned as cruel and unusual punishment violating the Eighth Amendment.[2]

Judge Brown also stated that "there is literally no evidence to support any of the charges against the 23 defendants."[3]

Second, Judge Brown stated that the basic question was not really one of "probable cause" or "fair trial" as considered by the other judges. Rather, the basic question to be considered was: Were we—the defendants— being deprived of a federal right under the thin veneer of legitimate criminal prosecution? For if the arrests were motivated only to punish us or inhibit us from participating in federally protected civil rights activities, then even the fact that we were being brought to trial—even if we were *acquitted*—was a violation of our rights and sufficient grounds for removal.

Judge Blown declared that the *motive behind the arrests* was the real consideration. It was true that we were not arrested at the time or place of the Mendenhall marches. So why were we arrested at all? What was the real motive of the officers behind the Highway 49 arrests and the Brandon beatings?

Judge Brown carefully catalogued all the crucial events of the night of February 7, 1970. And in doing so, he amassed a mountain of evidence that proved concern for law enforcement was a false motive. It also proved that hatred of civil rights workers, black or white, was the true motive.[4]

A vehicle carrying 18 blacks and 2 whites is stopped by a Mississippi Highway Patrolman a few hours after all of its occupants have participated in a peaceful march protesting racial discrimination in a nearby town. The Highway Patrol has kept the march under rigorous surveillance, and one of the vehicle's passengers notices a patrol car following them out of town.

After placing the driver of the vehicle in the patrol car, the officer asks him whether he and his passengers were participants in the demonstration. Upon receiving an affirmative answer, the patrolman threatens his subject, refers to the passengers as "niggers," and then radios for assistance. He calls to two of the vehicle's occupants who have gotten out, "You niggers, get back in that van." They do.

A few minutes later, between four and six patrol cars pull up, and the officers get out with drawn guns. Rather than ticketing the driver for a minor traffic offense, they arrest him and his passengers, handcuff them, and take them to jail. The driver claims that on the way he is beaten by a Highway Patrolman who has previously made threats to do precisely that, or worse, if he did not give up his civil rights activities.

Two of the Negro leaders of the protest march and a third black man, hearing of the arrests, go to the jail for the purpose of posting bond for those arrested. After parking in front of the jail and getting out of their car they are immediately arrested by 12 officers and taken inside. One of them is beaten on the way.

Once inside the jail two of the three prisoners and the driver arrested earlier are beaten with blackjacks, kicked, punched and verbally abused. During these proceedings the county sheriff forces the leader of the afternoon demonstration to read the demands made by his group, after telling him that he is a "smart nigger" and that his presence in the county constitutes "a whole new ballgame." The sheriff's son, who earlier participated in the Highway Patrol surveillance of the demonstration, is in the jail at the time, as are approximately 15 other law enforcement officers.

Subsequently two of the three organizers of the civil rights march have their heads shaved, and the sheriff himself pours moonshine whiskey over one of them. The prisoners are then kept in jail overnight and most are released the following day, although one—whose head has been split open with a blackjack—remains in jail all day Sunday and is finally released on Monday after posting the $5,000 bond demanded by the sheriff.

The State of Mississippi counters with the claim that it is all a coincidence and produces one witness—the sheriff—who denies that he struck anyone with a blackjack, a denial similar to one he has made six years earlier under similar circumstances. The sheriff says that after the civil rights leader swung at him he responded with two or three blows of his fist and that there was a general disturbance. Although he was in the room at the time the sheriff cannot say "who hit who." The sheriff denies that any of his men were drinking because he doesn't allow it. That sheriff admits that he personally poured moonshine whiskey on one of his prisoners after ordering their heads shaved. There are many other major and minor details, of course, but these are the highlights. My conception of a "routine traffic arrest" is at variance with the court's. As a Judge I cannot be blind to what everyone else can see.[5]

The traditional picture of Justice is a woman holding scales, blindfolded. The blindfold was meant to symbolize the ideal of impartiality for all courts. As far as it goes, it is a worthy ideal. But the judicial blindness that Judge Brown saw only served to promote the rigid system of injustice that characterized the state's legal system from bottom to top.

That blindness was evident at every stage of the state's proceedings. The trial judge who heard the original petition for removal "blindly" narrowed the scope of his inquiry by saying that there was probably good reason for a traffic arrest, without examining other relevant evidence pointing to a conspiracy of violence. Judge Brown also suggests deeper, heavier implications of that decision since the charges could have led to more than just imprisonment for myself and others. For once imprisoned, my life would be in real danger.

More than one "smart nigger" had faced the real possibility of physical violence and harm in prison—even death. My own experience while only under "detention" overnight, as well as the experience of other prisoners in state institutions, made this plain. My life would be at stake if I were ever put behind bars.

There was still one final chance for removal. Anyone whose case has been heard by a three-judge panel of the U.S. Court of

Appeals may petition for a rehearing *en bane*—a hearing before the entire 15 members of the court. We petitioned and were granted a rehearing on June 2, 1972.

My lawyers, Frank Parker and Constance Slaughter, researched a detailed 97-page brief and prepared oral arguments for this important rehearing. But a majority of the Appeals Court confirmed the original finding of the District Court. Petition denied.

In his dissent from the other justices, Judge Brown referred to a man and an event recorded in the book of Esther. After Haman was appointed chief counselor to the Persian king, Ahasuerus, he proposed a sweeping new law. All the members of the captive Jewish minority were to be branded as troublemakers and destroyed. No one was to be spared.

Mordecai, uncle of Queen Esther, heard of the decree and was grieved. He rent his clothes in public mourning for his people. He "put on sackcloth and ashes, and went out into the midst of the city, wailing with a loud and bitter cry; he went up to the entrance of the king's gate clothed with sackcloth" (Esther 4:1,2, *RSV*). And there he remained as a public plea for the fate of his people. Judge Brown revived this image of a people oppressed by the state of an earlier period and drew a parallel with the plight of our own people in twentieth-century Mississippi:

> Viewed from any realistic perspective this case marks a critical stage in the evolutionary development of Federal civil rights removal jurisdiction. Rev. Perkins is Mordecai at the Gate. His allegations and proof demand that we let him in.[6]

As in the aftermath of the Mendenhall trial, so in the final outcome of the Brandon arrests and beatings—a bit of legal horse trading provided our only out. Our lawyers had filed a suit against the state Highway Patrol for their brutality. That suit—though a perfectly fair and valid claim against the law officers—was dropped in return for the state's agreement not to prosecute the "resisting arrest" and other charges against the 23 defendants.

Again there was no real vindication or legal victory. Not one of those doing the beating was ever punished. But after two years of legal maneuvering, my lawyers advised me to accept this compromise. It was not a satisfactory ending, just the benefit of not being put behind bars. And, like I say, there's no telling what that might have meant.

So what comes out of all this? One of the things for Christian observers is that there are times when the biggest need is for information rather than exhortation. We need to know more about what really goes on before we solidify our theoretical ideas about what a Christian "ought" or "ought not" do.

Whether or not we admit it, our reading of biblical ethics is colored by our perception of the world around us. If we think that there are only a few "bad guys" such as burglars and murderers, and that all the given political, legal and economic structures around us are basically okay, then we are bound to read our Bibles in a certain way. We will assume that it tells us to "lay low," whether we are a part of the law or only under the law; that the person who speaks out is a rebellious agitator.

But that assumption can be badly shaken up by a good look at what happens to many people who are simply crushed by, rather than helped by, these social structures and institutions we take for granted. If sin can exist at every level of government, and in every human institution, then also the call to biblical justice in every corner of society must be sounded by those who claim a God of Justice as their Lord.

Judge Brown, we, like Mordecai, are still waiting at the gates of justice.

Stronger Than Ever

First the hot searing flash of open violence in early 1970. Then the dull, almost invisible glow in the background of legal appeals. They simmered on back burners, and occasionally someone stirred them up. Then they simmered some more.

It was not until June 2, 1972, going on two years after my first arrest, the one in Mendenhall, that the last legal word was handed down by the full U.S. Court of Appeals. And after this came that last compromise between my lawyers and the prosecutors.

But as I said, legal matters over those two years mostly simmered. And in between the stirrings, we mostly waited. But no way did we lack for things to do. Court or no court, we all had plenty to do.

Right after our release from the Brandon jail in February 1970, Doug Huemmer, Curry Brown and I did spend about a week in our lawyer's home in Jackson, getting our case together. And seeing Dr. Smith. Then we went back to Mendenhall.

There were a lot of new things going on in Mendenhall, but none of them could take the place of my Bible classes, youth meetings, fellowship groups—these activities I had started our work with. Along with these, I spent one or two days a week speaking and organizing sessions for various economic cooperatives under the sponsorship of the Federation of Southern Cooperatives.

The sober lawyers and the laughing youngsters. The business problems and the prayer times. The new things and the old. The Lord was helping me get them put together.

Like one Saturday in July 1970. The heat was so heavy it dripped from the trees. I was sitting in my little office in Mendenhall, getting things cleared up so I could go out to the ball park and watch the kids play. That meant a lot to me, sort of got my mind loosened up.

I love sports—and kids. And even though my family was broken, I was always a part of a family of kids who loved to play together.

But all at once, I felt tired. Clear worn out. More tired than I had ever felt before. I went to my office and lay down and just fell asleep. Right in the daytime.

But when I woke up I didn't feel rested. Just wobbly. Like I'd been sleeping for two or three days.

I don't remember how Sunday went by. But on Monday I convinced myself I felt able to make a trip I'd planned to Mound Bayou, a town in the delta, farther north. So I went.

There were some co-ops in Mound Bayou I had helped to organize. I observed their operations and talked with the managers. Then a lady on the board of directors fixed a nice dinner and invited us over.

But again I got so tired I could hardly sit up. And pains in my chest. I had to excuse myself and go lie down.

The next morning I checked in at the local health center, Tuft Medical Center, organized by blacks for blacks. The nurse found massively high blood pressure. And the machines hooked up to me ticked out on their charts that my heart was not functioning right— I had had a heart attack.

Dr. Joanne Roberts, a devout Catholic and one of the few white persons in the center, told me to go to bed. Right away. No traveling back to Mendenhall.

The days dragged by. One week. Two weeks. Maybe more. I began to feel stronger.

The doctors got their heads together, compared notes and said, "Okay, we'll let you go home now, if you want to."

I wanted to.

But it didn't last long. Back in Mendenhall I began to feel as sick as ever. So I went back to the medical center in Mound Bayou. For three weeks this time. Then back to Mendenhall again.

The fall of 1970 went by quietly. I was keeping a lot lighter schedule. But even so I began having stomach cramps.

In February 1971, one year after the Brandon beatings, I was on a speaking engagement in Ann Arbor, Michigan. By the time I made it back to the plane after the meeting, I was doubled up with cramps.

Ulcers.

It seemed like an awfully long night, flying back to Mississippi. Long and lonely. In the same Mound Bayou hospital, Dr. Harvey Saunders, a black doctor, took out about two-thirds of my stomach.

Three weeks more in the hospital, and then more rest and recovery with friends in Mound Bayou. That took until about the first of April.

Being hospitalized in Mound Bayou instead of in Mendenhall, I was far enough away from the action now to rest a little better. Not just away from people coming in all the time and needing to talk. But away from that feeling that just down the road a bit lay all sorts of unsettled problems and antagonisms. I guess God knew what I needed.

It's sort of hard, well, to get into words just what was going on inside me just then. There was just no other time in my whole life, either before or after I accepted Christ, that was so crucial to the whole meaning of my life, to the whole meaning of my work and to my thinking and being. My feelings about blacks and whites were, well, very intense.

Going up to Mound Bayou for all my medical treatment was an absolutely necessary part of this getting myself put together. You see, Mound Bayou was an all-black community. And that kind of separate existence among blacks was the only thing I could take during those months of pain.

You see, the pain in my heart was just as real, just as raw, as the pain in my stomach. Everything added up to the conviction that there was no justice at all. No justice at all for any black who wanted to stand up like a man in Mississippi.

It's hard to make all this clear or real to white people, but a lot of black people had come to this same point—feeling that there simply was no justice, no hope. All those radical anti-whites—Stokely Carmichael, Rap Brown, George Jackson, Eldridge Cleaver and the others—you heard about in the news, didn't invent the injustices they talked about. They saw and felt oppression in a thousand ways. And not always open brutality either. It's the system, the whole structure of economic and social cages that have neatly boxed the black man in so that "nice" people can join the oppression without getting their hands dirty—just by letting things run along.

When you see and feel that in your soul, you can't stand still. And if Christianity and white churches and white churchgoing businessmen, for all their revivals and preaching, seem to be propping up the system that degrades a man; if you've never in your life seen a *real* Christian, then you can see only one way to go. And a lot of blacks have gone that way. I don't mean just the loud black who mouths talk about revolution. I mean the black man who quietly builds his whole life apart from God. The white God.

And I was feeling the same pull, that pull to reject everything. My whole humanity, my whole self was telling me to reject everything I had once worked for. Not to give up. Oh, no! But to work for something different. To give up on whites and white

Christians and work only for me and mine. Work as competitor rather than co-worker.

Lying there in bed, I went over in my mind all the stages our work at VOC had gone through. I thought of the suffering and bitterness I'd unleashed by preaching what I thought the gospel included—the whole gospel. Yet from the very start our ministry in Mississippi faced threats and obstacles.

We had begun by preaching in the schools and speaking in big tent meetings all over the county. Then after a number of converts had joined us, we began a Bible institute. It was no graduate seminary, but it taught young black Christians to dig in to the Bible and find out for themselves what it says.

I had tried to involve white teachers in our work. A number were willing. And some had driven all the way from Jackson and Crystal Springs to lecture for us. But the Ku Klux Klan and intimidation had put a quick stop to that.

I thought a lot about our work as I lay there. I couldn't help it.

I remembered Dr. Odenwald. We had reached him. The gospel had penetrated his white attitudes. We fellowshipped together. And studied together. He was becoming excited about the possibilities of what might be.

But then Dr. Odenwald began to share out of his soul, exposing his racial attitudes. He was sure reasonable men, men of God, would accept what he had to say.

How wrong he was. And how wrong we were. Dr. Odenwald had unleashed a thousand hidden fears. He felt rejection. Brokenhearted and defeated, he killed himself. I thought a lot about Dr. Odenwald as I lay there. I couldn't help it.

Then came the civil rights movement. The movement stirred up a hurricane of white emotions and black expectations. And I couldn't stand apart from it. I had to practice what I preached—a whole gospel for the whole man.

I became involved. My family became involved. VOC became involved. Because we knew real change would not come for Mendenhall's blacks unless they gained their civil rights.

I headed up voter registration in our county. But where to register? We blacks had no spare buildings. And no white in Simpson County would rent space to the federal marshals who came in to register the blacks. So we registered blacks on the loading dock of the Post Office—the only federal property in town. And I organized the shuttle buses and vans for the registration effort.

We rode in fear. We registered in fear. And we voted in fear. Those black voting lists were carved out in fear.

Because of my work for civil rights, the hurricane blew hard against my family. Strange cars outside the house at night. Threatening phone calls in the wee hours of the morning. My wife and children lived in fear and anxiety—for me and for themselves.

I thought a lot about a lot of things as I lay there. I couldn't help it.

What was the point of it all? Was I accomplishing anything? Was I bringing good news to the people of Mendenhall? Or was I only creating more hatred and violence—and hurting more people?

I thought with real sadness of the gospel I believed in with all my heart. The gospel that says in Christ there is no black or white. I believed that gospel was powerful enough to shatter even the hatred of Mendenhall. But I had not seen it. Especially in the churches.

On April 3, 1970—a month after my trial in Mendenhall—the state legislature repealed both statutory prohibitions against racial integration and the criminal laws providing for racially segregated public facilities. Restaurants, schools, offices—even in Mississippi, these places were starting to integrate. But where was there an integrated church?

Tragically, but true—churchgoers in America are the slowest to change. So what was the future of the whole concept of integration in Mendenhall? In Mississippi?

Yes, I thought a lot about the church and integration as I lay there. I couldn't help it.

Day after day, I would lie there and wonder what it was all worth. Dr. Saunders did a lot for me. And so did Dr. Roberts. Dr. Roberts was one of the few white persons I had contact with at that time, and she, well, she met me on the level of my humanity and not just on the theological level preferred by so many church folks. Those two doctors saw me through that crisis, a battle that could have destroyed me as much as any physical crisis.

Hope began flickering anew in my heart and mind. Images of hope. One was the impact we'd had on the young people of Mendenhall. Our first converts were now away at college, getting trained so they could return to teach others.

Spencer, my own son, had been one of the first to integrate Mendenhall's high school, one of a few blacks among 500 whites. He spent two terribly lonely years in that school. But he'd survived. In this family, in the VOC community, he had found the strength to survive. And already scores of others were now integrating schools—and surviving.

Slowly but surely, change was coming. The gospel was bringing changes. And I was a part of this change. Other images also gave hope. I knew there were whites who *did* care. There were whites who were supporting the work every month. White Christian doctors were treating me now and nursing me back to health. A white lawyer was preparing my legal case. White college graduates were working for VOC and earning less than $100 a month. Doug Huemmer and Ira Freshman, both whites, had endured the Brandon beatings and arrests along with the black victims.

God was showing me something, telling me something. There were blacks who had accepted our message. Who had embraced the gospel. Who now knew dignity. Who now walked taller than before.

And there were whites who believed in justice. Who lived love. Who shared themselves. Who joined our community.

I began to see with horror how hate could destroy me—destroy me more devastatingly and suddenly than any destruction I could bring on those who had wronged me. I could try and fight back, as many of my brothers had done. But if I did, how would I be different from the whites who hate?

And where would hating get me? Anyone can hate. This whole business of hating and hating back. It's what keeps the vicious circle of racism going.

The Spirit of God worked on me as I lay in that bed. An image formed in my mind. The image of the cross—Christ on the cross. It blotted out everything else in my mind.

This Jesus knew what I had suffered. He understood. And He cared. Because He had experienced it all Himself.

This Jesus, this One who had brought good news directly from God in heaven, had lived what He preached. Yet He was arrested and falsely accused. Like me, He went through an unjust trial. He also faced a lynch mob and got beaten. But even more than that, He was nailed to rough wooden planks and killed. Killed like a common criminal.

At the crucial moment, it seemed to Jesus that even God Himself had deserted Him. The suffering was so great, He cried out in agony. He was dying.

But when He looked at that mob that had lynched Him, He didn't hate them. He loved them. He forgave them. And He prayed God to forgive them. "Father, forgive these people, for they don't know what they are doing."

His enemies hated. But Jesus forgave. I couldn't get away from that.

The Spirit of God kept working on me and in me until I could say with Jesus, "I forgive them, too." I promised Him that I would "return good for evil," not evil for evil. And He gave me the love I knew I would need to fulfill His command to me of "love your enemy."

Because of Christ, God Himself met me and healed my heart and mind with His love. I knew then what Paul meant when he wrote:

> Who shall separate us from the love of Christ? shall tribulation, or distress, or persecution, or famine, or nakedness, or peril, or sword? Nay, in all these things we are more than conquerors through him that loved us. For I am persuaded, that neither death, nor life, nor angels, nor principalities, nor powers, nor things present, nor things to come, nor height, nor depth, nor any other creature, shall be able to separate us from the love of God, which is in Christ Jesus our Lord (Rom. 8:35,37-39).

The Spirit of God helped me to really believe what I had so often professed, that only in the love of Christ is there any hope for me, or for those I had once worked so hard for. After that, God gave me the strength and motivation to rise up out of my bed and return to Mendenhall and spread a little more of His love around.

Oh, I know man is bad—depraved. There's something built into him that makes him want to be superior. If the black man had the advantage, he'd be just as bad, just as bad. So I can't hate the white man.

The problem is spiritual: black or white, we all need to be born again.

It's a profound, mysterious truth—Jesus' concept of love overpowering hate. I may not see its victory in my lifetime. But I know it's true.

I know it's true, because it happened to me. On that bed, full of bruises and stitches—God made it true in me. He washed my hatred away and replaced it with a love for the white man in rural Mississippi.

I felt strong again. Stronger than ever. What doesn't destroy me makes me stronger.

I know it's true.

Because it happened to me.

The People of God

Something else happened to me in the hospital. God showed me I couldn't do everything alone. I couldn't be the big strong superman showing the blacks the way to the Promised Land.

I needed to build a community spirit. I needed to learn to lean on people. We had to come together. We had to become God's people—His Church—for anything good to happen in Mendenhall. We had to teach blacks that the answer is not in following the white man's way of competition and power. We had to need each other.

As I lay on my bed and thought and prayed over this, all the scars and hurts of the past seemed to fade away. I got another transfusion of God's hope. For a moment, I had seen my pain as the violent, convulsive end to everything for which I had worked.

But God had entered me and made me see it as the stinging, bittersweet beginning to everything He was going to do in Mendenhall. We were just getting underway.

So I came out of that long stay in Tufts Medical Center determined not only to keep on with the work, but also able to see more clearly than ever what was the true heart of our work. Groups have always seemed to me the best way to go about getting things done, but now I was seeing more clearly than ever how important it is for Christians to be the *people* of God, and not just a collection of individual believers who gather weekly for the convenience of joint worship on Sunday.

To develop the Christian community as a group that could show love within itself and to the world would be creating a new entity that was more than the sum of the individual Christians. The community's existence itself, as a structure, would open up so many new channels of strength and witness. Individual hero-ism and suffering, though always needed at times of crisis, would not be able to inflict such terrible isolation on the individuals who lived and breathed in a brotherhood of intertwined lives.

Much of this had already been in the making, but I now saw the need for it in brighter focus. June 1971 saw one part of that dream materialize. Dolphus Weary, who had been associated with the work from teenage follower through college and grad-uate study, had now returned to Mendenhall. He was able to take over the day-by-day responsibilities as executive director of the Voice of Calvary. He took over the tutoring program and helped expand the Bible classes to five evenings a week. Freed of some of the daily burden, I was now able to work more on fund-raising and promoting new projects.

There was plenty of need for new funds. The expanded tutoring program was only one project. The most visible project of 1972 was the new vocational workshop and gym that we designed ourselves. The new combination building, dedicated to the new generation of black youth, is named the R. A. Buckley Christian Youth Center, after a man who has been one of the staunchest supporters of the younger generation—R. A. Buckley, now 87 years old. Out of a life of struggle and deep devotion, R. A. Buckley has become one of my closest friends and advisers.

Everyone at VOC pitched in to help with the building—we put in the foundation ourselves, then a contractor put up the steel framework and then we built the cement block walls. What was built during those months was more than just a building. Conflicts, fears and uncertainties had taken their toll, but the physical labor on a project of our own helped restore our sense of accomplishment and channeled bitterness into building.

With the gym built we began to work on another project that grew out of the great tornado of 1969 that had devastated parts of Simpson County and that had followed in the wake of Hurricane Camille. In that emergency, the Voice of Calvary helped provide food and clothing for the destitute. And our VOC program—including the co-ops and the immediate relief programs—impressed such outside observers as *Jet* magazine and presidential assistant Robert Brown, sent down here to observe the damage and relief efforts.

So after the tornado, the Community Education Extension, under a research grant, surveyed the area, examining not only storm damage, but overall health conditions. Vera Mae was a surveyor for Simpson County. The project continued from late 1969 to the time of the Brandon incident in February 1970. The survey gave alarming confirmation to what many of the local people already knew: poor health walked hand in hand with poverty through Simpson County.

And not only poor health, but poor health care. The only white doctors who would treat blacks had separate waiting rooms for blacks and whites. On one side of the wall, in a carpeted, furnished waiting room, whites were treated immediately. And only after all the white patients were treated, would the doctor see some blacks from the other side. To meet this urgent need, VOC envisaged a health center where every black would be treated with respect.

Then in the fall of 1972, Erv and Joan Huston arrived to join the staff. Erv had his degree from Bethany Seminary and Joan was a registered nurse. They joined in the new effort, which extended through 1973, of organizing a local cooperative health center. The idea was not simply to erect a free, mission-style health clinic, but to provide health care—the most expensive of necessities—through the cooperative efforts of the people themselves.

A model for cooperatives exists, of course, in the Bible. Communitywide responsibility was a basic characteristic of the Old Testament Jews, but it functioned in a community where the economic system, the political system, the religious organization—every aspect of life—covered the same group of individuals. That way a cooperative effort to meet one particular need could be reinforced by the other structures of Jewish society. But in twentieth-century America, or in any other complex industrialized society, a small community is simply not locked into the larger systems of banking, education, government or industry that determine its quality of life—or the lack of it. And continuous needs of certain segments of our society are the result of this. Something is out of whack in our society. For people ought to be able to provide their own needs. When will and effort are organized and still fall short, this means only that the resources needed are locked up somewhere. And no amount of talk about "private property" or "free enterprise" will ever touch the real moral issue of our responsibility to others.

So it is no contradiction of the co-op principle to say that co-ops among the have-nots, though organized on the self-help principle, often need specific outside assistance. To recognize this will not only help specific co-op ventures, like our health co-op, but will open eyes to the larger goal of making entire communities more economically viable.

So the year 1973 saw the opening of the health center, with a key priority being a doctor. Dr. Kevin Lake from Pasadena, California, came to open the clinic. Then for several months, Dr. Charles Fraley served in the clinic before his scheduled departure for Africa with the Africa Inland Mission. On May 14, 1974, the VOC community bade him a reluctant good-bye. Dr.

Henry Loewen from Kansas came for one month. But after him, there was no other doctor in sight. The clinic and pharmacy had to be closed, even before the new building had been completely finished inside.

While prayers continued for a permanent doctor, other projects progressed. New X-ray equipment worth $13,000, paid for in large and small donations from the community and around the country, was being installed. As the warm spring ripened, so did the hope of somehow, somewhere finding a new doctor.

Friday, April 12, was to be a big day—the official dedication of the new X-ray equipment. But Thursday night it began to rain. And Friday morning saw no letup as sodden clouds continued to unload torrents all over south-central Mississippi.

The black section of Mendenhall is on the low edge of town, so Dolphus Weary, sensing disaster, began mobilizing the Voice of Calvary staff. They took all movable equipment and set it as high as possible.

Surely the rain would ease off any time now. But the morning wore on without a letup in the rain. Nobody could remember when it had rained that hard before.

The staff got busy again. They began moving furniture and people out of low-lying homes to higher ground. And struggling through water already knee-deep by early afternoon.

Later we heard that it rained a record-breaking 15 inches in 30 hours. From where he stood on an embankment above the crest of the flood, Dolphus watched the angry waters push through the youth center. Through the tutorial school. Through the health center where our yet undedicated X-ray sat. A short distance away, the ravaging floodwaters tore away the fence around his yard and pushed higher and deeper through the rooms of his house.

The dedication service had been set for four that afternoon. But about two in the afternoon Dolphus called me at the Jackson office and broke the news to me. I phoned Vera Mae at home and told her what had happened. Then I drove down to Mendenhall and joined Dolphus.

There wasn't much to say. As we stood there, we saw the dreams of a lifetime—years of sweat, labor and laughter—dissolve inch by inch. Minute by minute. They just dissolved and floated away. God forgive us for wondering why.

The havoc was beyond description. And so many of the townspeople were just paralyzed by their losses. For a person whose whole life is wrapped up in his possessions—his house or his car or anything else that can be lost—physical loss is the same as losing part of himself.

But God had given us at Voice of Calvary something that could not be lost. Something no flood could destroy. We felt God at this moment called us to face again the same kind of challenge we had lived with for 14 years: to find needs and to fill them in the name of Christ. Our staff met together for prayer and "What next?" ideas. And as we did so, I reminded them that, now more than ever, the unity I had been calling for was an absolute necessity for the whole community.

So late that night, black people met to share their despairs and to develop a strategy for survival. Again, prayer for unity was the key as I opened the meeting. With Dolphus Weary as chairman, the Community Disaster Committee was formed.

Within 24 hours the committee had drawn up a survey form, and had surveyed the total disaster area even before the Red Cross could get there. The unity of effort even crossed racial lines as the flood victims, mostly black, called upon the mayor of Mendenhall, Ray Layton, to represent their needs to the governor. Layton himself later said that he was appointed chairman of the county's disaster areas primarily because of the way the people of his own town had met the challenge.

The slow cleanup job began as the flood water began to sub-side. There was $8,500 worth of damage to the X-ray equipment. That could eventually be restored.

But could the spirit of the community be restored? Yes, for despite our anguish we saw that the Christian sense of community we had worked and prayed for had stood solid when everything else had melted away. The disaster had not taken with it our assurance of God's presence and the confidence that He does, indeed, protect His own.

And on the horizon there were other answers to prayer. In Jackson, plans were being laid for a Bible institute that would unite biblical training for young people with the understanding of Christian responsibility in society that I had been piecing together during 15 years of struggle. As I told the staff, we'd been busy doing a lot of things during these years, but we hadn't always managed to put across what it was we were trying to do. Those on the outside, and even the volunteers who would come for a few weeks of work, often didn't see beyond the bricks and the shovels. Communication had been one of our biggest problems.

So, in October 1974, the Jackson Bible Institute opened with four classes in the large house that also contains the offices of our other projects. Here young blacks—and whites—can grapple with the issues of Christian community and find significance in their own world.

And in that same month came another breakthrough. A young pediatrician, Dr. Eugene McCarty of Colorado Springs, Colorado, came to visit. He and his wife, Joanne, looked over the vacant health center and met the people in Mendenhall.

For several evenings we talked far into the night. Then on Sunday, October 13, during the worship service in Mendenhall, the slender, soft-spoken doctor stood up and told us, "My wife and I are convicted by what the Lord is doing here, and we want to respond by saying that we would like to become a part of your ministry, if you decide to have us."

There was shouting and crying in the service that day. Here was the answer to prayers of people all over the county, prayers for a permanent doctor. But it was more than that, too. For, despite the crucial need for health care, it was not the entirety of our vision. The coming of a doctor was a symbol of other things beyond that event.

The growing conviction of the need for a living Christian community with economic and social cohesion was met in the fact that Dr. McCarty was not just volunteering to come at a fraction of his former income on a short-term basis. He would become a part of that world.

Dr. McCarty's life, then, would not be patterned in the usual segmented style our technological world has come to accept as normal. In that world, a man has only partial interaction with others and in specialized roles: as professional, as church member, as father, as neighbor, in differing circles that sometimes touch but never overlap completely. So, more than getting a doctor, the new developments were a further strengthening of the Christian community, the Christian reality of fellowship for which I was devoting my entire life. For me, a man who had come close to death, that one further step of life for the community, partial though it was, still was a deep reminder that the fellowship of the gospel was indeed worthy of every struggle, every effort of a man's life.

This man's life is firmly committed to the ministry of the gospel in Mississippi. I know why my Lord saved me. And I know why He led me here. In a land where hatred once reigned unchallenged, I have already seen God in His glory carve out a pocket of love.

Where there was despair, there is now hope. Where there was oppression, there is now opportunity. Where there was defeat, there is now purpose. And where there was weakness, there is now strength—a strength that comes only from God. I face the future buoyant in the courage and confidence born of faith in Jesus Christ alone. "For I know whom I have believed, and am persuaded that he is able to keep that which I have committed unto him against that day" (2 Tim. 1:12).

And until "that day," the Voice of Calvary will continue to be a voice of Christ in Mississippi.

Let Justice Roll On

By Elizabeth Perkins

I was just a little girl when Regal first published this book. I remember spending endless hours at a friend's cabin, playing outside by the artesian well while my father was inside remembering, recreating and writing about the dramatic events of his own life, the civil rights movement and all that God had done. I had a vague sense of its importance, but little did I know then how much *Let Justice Roll Down* would impact so many lives, including my own.

By the time this book was complete, Daddy and many others who came out of the Civil Rights movement had come to see that justice was not simply a physical condition or a set of laws, but it really was an economic issue—especially the justice that affected us as African-Americans living in the South. Because our ancestors had come over to America as slaves, the question of economic empowerment was large. (This point about justice being an economic issue is something Daddy would later discuss with President George W. Bush and a principle he would apply while serving on several presidential commissions.) My father's words:

> The Civil Rights Movement succeeded in the sense that it removed those laws that were barriers. It broke down

the walls of educational opportunity, economic opportunity and political opportunity. By electing black officials, the fear that went with segregation is pretty well gone.

But if we look at justice as an economic issue—especially the injustice of slavery that resulted in a lack of ownership, job opportunity and education—we haven't made much headway. We've got a few more rich blacks, but the system is still a problem for most.

If black folks were getting 10 percent justice in the '60s, they're getting 30 percent or 40 percent now. So there has been almost triple the amount of freedom. There has been massive progress. But if we talk in terms of justice as equality, we're still talking about an imbalance.

One of the most popular ways to respond to economic injustice is through better education. The idea is that if people get solid training, they can get jobs. Of course, back then everyone could see that African-Americans were deprived of their education and deprived of the good jobs. Even after the forced integration of the schools, African-Americans were just maintaining, not improving.

My father and others saw that while African-Americans had been taught the basics: reading, writing and speaking (important skills that made them better servants), our people did not understand how the social economic system worked. They didn't know how to develop resources, accumulate assets or manage finances. Without these basics, how could they ever run their own businesses? How could they ever be empowered? Of course, getting better education is important—and through the years my father has started many schools and training programs. But getting hands-on experience was vital.

The cooperative movement that Daddy launched in Mendenhall gave people hope and understanding. It also gave them experience. They started a thrift store, a health clinic and many other enterprises.

The health clinic not only filled a need but it was also very symbolic. In 1973, the ministry acquired a medical building in downtown Mendenhall, strategically located across from the courthouse. The medical building had previously been segregated, with separate entrances and waiting rooms for whites and coloreds. One time when my brother Phillip was sick, my father had to take him to the health center, enter through the coloreds-only door and wait all day before seeing a doctor. After the ministry acquired the building, Daddy was there with a sledgehammer knocking down the wall that had separated the waiting rooms. Justice was rolling on.

Most of the enterprises in Mendenhall and nearby have since closed. As time went on, they were not able to compete with Wal-Mart, Target and the other large chains—yet what emerged from the movement was a greater understanding of economics among African-Americans. People who had been deprived for so long now knew how to read a financial statement, how the stock market worked and how to run a business.

My father tells me that when he now visits Mendenhall and other Mississippi towns, the people who are the most advantaged today are those who were in the cooperative movement. One of the most successful of them is a lawyer named Isaac K. Byrd, who as a kid had marched with Daddy in Mendenhall.

So much has happened in the years since *Let Justice Roll Down* was written. Recounting it all would fill the pages of many books—and hopefully Daddy will soon write his memoirs. So in this short postscript, rather than attempt to include every detail, I have selected a few significant stories.

In 1972, we moved from Mendenhall about 34 miles north to Jackson, Mississippi. The city was larger and the needs greater, so my father founded Voice of Calvary Ministries. As in Mendenhall, he started cooperatives and a church. He launched a study center, helped start the Southern Cooperative Development Fund (a bank) and the People's Development Incorporated, which helped with housing needs. And it was here that he came up with the strategy to seed every neighborhood with two or three Christian families as a way to bring about community change.

In Jackson, my father would set up a tent and preach at outdoor meetings. The whole neighborhood would come. Now called the Lynch Street Festival, it became a regular event.

To this day, Daddy will reflect and think deeply when he recalls a white police officer who came regularly to the tent meetings. The officer's name was King. Remember, it was white police officers like King who had beaten Daddy and the others in Brandon. It was a white marshal who had killed Daddy's brother. And it was white police officers who routinely took advantage of their positions of power over colored people. So it wasn't so easy or natural to have one come to our tent.

At first Officer King would just stand in the back, and then he started talking with my father about how something needed to be done about the crime in the neighborhood. My father remembers Officer King this way:

> He looked like the stereotypical Mississippi policeman, so I figured he was probably racist. It was hard for me to get past that. But he started supporting so much of what we were doing. He showed me a deep, deep respect and affirmed me as a human being. His coming there to me finally broke through. He became my friend, and undermined my attitude so that I could no longer look at all

policemen as evil. He started a healing process that had me coming out from my own sin, out of my own malice. God used that white policeman to start a healing in me.

This is what makes the gospel so unique. It's how beautiful are the feet of him who brings it—that's the lowest part of the body. The purpose of the gospel is to burn through racial and social barriers. And how beautiful are the feet of those who carry that gospel. It's not just tell, tell, tell—it's love. It is the creative witness and the manifestation of that witness. Officer King loved his job, he loved me because of what I was doing and he showed me his love by his presence. It was him who brought the good news to me.

Reconciliation for Officer King meant that this old black preacher was doing something in the community that nobody else was doing. You see, some of the elderly white women who still lived in the neighborhood were coming to the tent meetings and so were the blacks. I think Officer King saw that something was happening— that he needed me and I needed him. When we need each other's service we have meaning to each other. And when we understand the gospel, we see each other as equal. That's reconciliation.

Not long after that, Mississippi Governor William Winter and Jackson Mayor Dale Danks were present to help dedicate the Voice of Calvary Health Center in Jackson—something that would have been unthinkable just a few years earlier. Now that's reconciliation.

Another few years, and the Jackson newspaper—*The Clarion-Ledger*—published an article about two men who helped shape Mississippi: Daddy and Klansman Tommy Tarrants. The story is so powerful the article was reproduced and distributed in Mississippi's public schools, even in Mendenhall.

How did my father overcome racism? He tells it best:

> People always ask me how I overcame racism and big-otry. At least the process in my life that has helped me to overcome it has been the people and the quality of my Christian friends who have embraced me and loved me. People remove racism. Good overcomes evil. In my deep-est time of pain and sorrow and conflict, God has always brought somebody into my life who has loved me and embraced me at the time when it would have felt better to hate.

In 1980, Daddy took my brothers Spencer and Derek to Kenya for 32 days. They visited villages and saw the Kenyans' spirit of family and community—qualities that most African-Americans did not have. Especially my brothers came back with a renewed pride in our African heritage, and wanted to bring the sense of community spirit back to Mississippi. Out of that came the Harambee School of Business, complete with an after-school curriculum— from "Harambee nyio," a Swahili chant that means "let's get together and push."

It was amazing to see how what started in Mississippi would also have an impact in Southern California and beyond. In 1982, my parents returned to the West Coast—of course, they chose to live on a street known for its cocaine dealers and stabbings. They called their work the Harambee Christian Family Center.

As my father listened to the people in the neighborhood, he found that the needs were different here than in rural Mississippi. In Pasadena, many of the young kids had only one parent living at home. Gangs and drug dealers were picking up children at an early age. Many dropped out of school and got in trouble with the law.

Harambee started a tutoring program in the evening. It was overwhelming in terms of the number of people who came. Eventually we bought three former crack houses and now use them for ministry. We also started business clubs and eventually a prep school. The idea was to raise up some of the talented kids who could then change the neighborhood.

My father's memoirs will no doubt contain page after page of great stories from Pasadena, including how the movement that began in rural Mississippi expanded around the nation and the world. In 1989, to help extend the vision, my father and like-minded people formed the Christian Community Development Association. I will let him explain:

> At CCDA we see ourselves as turning this pyramid of power upside down. What we mean by that is that our traditional American way of power has everything starting at the bottom with the vast poor, and it goes up like a pyramid to the working middleclass, then the upper middleclass, then the rich and then the super rich. Going up the pyramid, there are fewer and fewer people—only a very few billionaires. We would like to see the pyramid turn upside down. That's what CCDA is about.

Early one morning, not long ago, my father and I were having a time of prayer and Bible study. We were reading from the Gospel of John, the part where on the cross Jesus turned to John and said, "Take care of my mother." John calls himself "that disciple whom Jesus loved." I am not sure why, but I turned to Daddy and said, "Do you realize that that's your name?"

My father's mother had died just after he was born. As we sat with our Bibles still open to the Gospel of John, I could see the emotion well up in his eyes and I knew he was thinking, *People say that when my mother was on her bed, sick and dying, I was still sucking on her breast. I was probably taking the nutrition that would have kept her alive. I was probably sucking the best nutrition right out.*

Suddenly my father jumped to his feet, looked at me and said, "You know, I killed my mother."

I stood up, just put my arms around him and assured him, "You didn't kill your mother. Your mother was doing exactly what she would have wanted to do. Her death would have been just exactly what she would have wanted to happen, that you would live."

Another loss shook my father. My oldest brother Spencer died of a heart attack in 1998 at age 44. Daddy says Spencer died of a broken heart. I suppose that could be true if you look at how it was always so difficult for Spencer to get the resources to fulfill his dreams. But there is another way to look at it, too.

Spencer was the All-American boy: the first African-American to lead the Mendenhall High School basketball team to a state championship; one of the first African-Americans to graduate from Belhaven College. He married young, started a Christian community here in Jackson and published *Urban Family Magazine*. His dreams were big—no surprise, he was my father's son.

My father tells what happened at the hospital where Spencer couldn't be revived:

> I drove behind the ambulance and got to the hospital just as they took him into the room. The doctors stayed with him for about 20 minutes, but could not save him.
>
> A verse went through my mind, *But if it die, it'll bring forth more fruit.* So I said, "God, I would like to give my son back to You tonight as a seed of reconciliation. And

that from this seed would grow many others. It would sprout all over this nation and my son's seed would not have been in vain." I did that. I felt pretty good about it. But as time went on, I began to see that that was actually going to happen.

I think this might be what drives me forward. So I decided to call our new work in Jackson the Spencer Perkins Center for Reconciliation and Youth Development. In a way, this prayer and God's answer have saved me from grief, especially when I'm out in the yard pulling up weeds or sweeping a sidewalk. When I'm out working, I think about him and how his seed is bearing fruit.

Indeed, John Perkins has faced the challenges of his day head on. He was involved in the civil rights movement, championed the Voter's Rights Act, stood up to the apartheid system in the South and confronted myriad other social injustices—even risking his status in the community, his own well being and his family's future.

As my father has forged ahead, he has been a spiritual father to thousands of people—not only those in his generation, but also to so many who have followed. He believes so much in this new generation that he is now lifting us onto his shoulders so we can get a better view and begin to face the challenges of our day.

As my biological daddy and spiritual mentor, he has allowed me to be a part of an amazing, incredible example of a ministry. Because of him, I dream bigger. As members of the next generation of emerging leaders, we must exercise a great amount of patience and love and recognize we are standing on the shoulders of those who have gone before us. From this vantage point, we can look ahead to see the mountains and the valleys. While still standing on their shoulders, we can look behind and see the valleys they had to go through. It reminds me of the Negro National Anthem, "Lift Every Voice and Sing." The end of the second verse goes like this:

> We have come over a way that with tears has been
> watered
> We have come, treading our path through the blood of
> the slaughtered;
> Out from the gloomy past
> Till now we stand at last
> Where the white gleam of our bright star is cast.

My daddy's vision of seeing justice roll down for all has become my vision. It has become my generation's responsibility to carry on the torch of racial reconciliation and Christian community development. Shane Claiborne (who wrote the foreword to this classic edition), I and others of our generation gladly accept this challenge.

Under our watch it is our responsibility to honor those who have come before us and to build on what we have been given. I close by paraphrasing Abraham Lincoln's Gettysburg address:

> We the people of this new generation highly resolve that
> those who sacrificed before us shall not have sacrificed
> in vain. Let justice roll on.

Endnotes

Chapter 13: The Whole Gospel

1. Neil R. McMillan, "The Development of Civil Rights: 1956-1970," *A History of Mississippi*, ed. Richard Aubrey McLemore, vol. 2 (Hattiesburg, MI: University and College Press of Mississippi, 1973), p. 156.

Chapter 17: Green Power!

1. "On each occasion the demonstrators were under the close surveillance of numerous uniformed and plainclothes officers of the Mississippi Highway Patrol, who followed each march and took pictures of the participants with motion picture and still cameras." *Perkins* v. *State of Mississippi*, 455 Federal Reporter, 2nd series (1972), p. 14.

Chapter 18: Ambush!

1. "Sam Ivy, the director of the Identification Bureau of the Highway Patrol, testified that he had dispatched at least two of his 15 agents to Mendenhall to cover the February protest activities, while Inspector Lloyd Jones, the officer in charge of the uniformed patrolmen of the Jackson Division, stated that at least six of his men were on duty at that time, including a specially trained photographer and an 'electronics surveillance man.' The officers employed a number of devices for identifying the leaders and participants in the marches, either by cross-checking with each other or by verifying vehicle registrations, and during the demonstrations they operated radar and VASCAR speed traps on the highway leading in and out of Mendenhall.

   "Inspector Ivy also testified that the Highway Patrol maintained a permanent file on investigations involving the Mendenhall civil rights movement." *Perkins* v. *State of Mississippi*, 455 Federal Reporter, 2nd Series (1972), p. 14.

2. *Perkins* v. *State of Mississippi*, pp. 14-15.

3. *Perkins* v. *State of Mississippi*, p. 15.

4. *Perkins* v. *State of Mississippi*, p. 8. "Baldwin further testified that he had received no radio message to stop the van. It was not until all the individuals had gotten out of the van that he recognized he had stopped people associated with the demonstrations in Mendenhall." *Perkins v. State of Mississippi*, p. 9.

   Yet "the official radio log of the Mississippi Highway Patrol for February 7, 1970, contains an entry pertaining to a vehicle license check radioed to the scene of the arrests: 'R/6152770 (panel truck) involved in demonstration.'" *Perkins* v. *State of Mississippi,* p. 17.

5. *Perkins* v. *State of Mississippi,* p. 15.
6. *Perkins* v. *State of Mississippi,* p. 15.
7. *Perkins* v. *State of Mississippi,* p. 8.
8. *Perkins* v. *State of Mississippi,* p. 15. "The State did not attempt to impeach or refute this evidence with the testimony of Patrolman Baldwin. It is uncontradicted." *Perkins* v. *State of Mississippi,* p. 15. "Baldwin admitted under oath that in making the call he might have said, 'I've got a truck load of niggers and there's a white with them.'" *Perkins v. State of Mississippi,* p. 15.
9. *Perkins v. State of Mississippi,* p. 15.
10. *Perkins v. State of Mississippi,* p. 9.
11. "In his testimony Patrolman Baldwin never managed to satisfactorily account for the arrest of the 19 passengers:

> "Q. 'Officer, why did you arrest the people inside the van?'
> "A. 'Well they wanted to go.'
> "Q. 'Did every one of them indicate that they wanted you to place them under arrest?'
> "A. 'Sir?'
> "Q. 'Did every one of them come up to you and say, "Officer, I would like to be arrested." Is that a fact?'
> "A. 'The statement was made that one person wasn't going unless all went.'
> "Q. 'One person made that statement?"
> "A. 'Yes.'
> "Q. 'Nobody else made that statement?"
> "A. 'I couldn't say.'
> "Q. 'And on the basis of that statement, you arrested them all, is that right?'
> "A. 'Yes, sir.'" *Perkins v. State of Mississippi,* pp. 15-16.

12. *Perkins v. State of Mississippi,* p. 16.
13. *Perkins v. State of Mississippi,* p. 16.
14. *Perkins v. State of Mississippi,* p. 16. "Although Officer Thames was available to testify, the State did not call him. Huemmer's testimony is uncontradicted." *Perkins v. State of Mississippi,* p. 16.
15. "This is the Court's second encounter with this individual. The first was *United States v. Edwards,* 5th Cir., 1964, 333 F. 2d 575, in which the Department of Justice sought an injunction under the Civil Rights Act of 1957 to restrain his interference with the Federally protected right to vote after he beat up a black citizen waiting to register in the Rankin County courthouse. Affirming the District Court's denial of injunctive relief on the theory that

the defendant had not engaged in a continuing and systematic course of intimidation, the Court referred to the incident as an 'isolated occurrence' and accepted the finding that 'there was no reasonable justification to believe that such an incident would ever occur again.' 333 F.2d at 577.

"As a dissenting member of that panel my conclusion then was that the affair was 'no case of isolated momentary violence." 333. F.2d at 581. Implicit was my conviction that such flagrantly lawless conduct would be repeated and that injunctive relief was imperative. Now, more than seven years later, this record—even when read most favorable to the sheriff—bears out my prediction." *Perkins v. State of Mississippi*, p. 18.

16. *Perkins v. State of Mississippi*, p. 17.
17. *Perkins v. State of Mississippi*, p. 17. "Neither Thames nor anyone else contradicted this testimony." *Perkins v. State of Mississippi*, p. 17.
18. "The sheriff testified that Rev. Perkins swung at him for no apparent reason and that he responded by hitting him two or three times with his fist. For some unexplained reason neither Rev. Perkins nor any of the other prisoners were charged with assaulting the sheriff or any other officer." *Perkins v. State of Mississippi*, p. 18.
19. *Perkins v. State of Mississippi*, p. 18. (Emphasis added.)
20. *Perkins v. State of Mississippi*, pp. 9, 19.
21. *Perkins v. State of Mississippi*, p. 20.
22. *Perkins v. State of Mississippi*, p. 19.
23. *Perkins* v. *State of Mississippi*, p. 19.
24. *Perkins v. State of Mississippi*, pp. 18-19.

Chapter 19: Beyond Brandon

1. "Hotheads and Professionals," *Time* (August 10, 1970), pp. 42-43.
2. "Advocacy of social equality between the white and black races—the activity involved in the Mendenhall demonstrations and sheltered against prosecution by Title 1 of the Civil Rights Act of 1968—is a criminal offense in Mississippi. On the date of the events in question all Mississippi law enforcement officers were under a statutory duty imposed by the State Legislature to 'lawfully' prohibit any attempt to cause 'a mixing or integration of the white and Negro races in public schools, public parks, public waiting rooms, public places of amusement, recreation or assembly' in the State." *Perkins v. State of Mississippi*, p. 48.
3. "'We find that terror hangs over the Negro in Mississippi and is an expectancy for those who refuse to accept their color as a badge of inferiority.' Report of the Mississippi Advisory Commission to the U.S. Commission on Civil Rights, Administration of Justice in Mississippi 23 (1963)." *Perkins v. State of Mississippi*, p. 49.

Chapter 20: Mississippi Justice

1. Not until 1975 in Mississippi were justices of the peace even required to be high school graduates.

Chapter 21: At the Gates of Justice

1. "At the hearing in the District Court the petitioners presented overwhelming proof that all of the charges pending against them are totally without foundation. Rather than attempting to counter this massive barrage of testimony, the State of Mississippi stood virtually mute. Under such circumstances silence by itself constitutes evidence of the most convincing character." *Perkins v. State of Mississippi,* p. 51.

   "The District Court made no explicit findings with respect to the credibility of any of the witnesses . . . Instead, relying entirely upon findings of probable cause for the arrests, without referring specifically to any of the petitioners' testimony regarding their treatment on Highway 49 and at the Rankin County jail, and bypassing entirely the allegations in the removal petition that the prosecutions were groundless and instituted solely for the purpose of intimidating the defendants because of their previous exercise of . . . rights, the District Court simply remanded on the basis of a general conclusory finding that the defendants 'were not arrested by these officers for doing anything which they had a federal right to do.' The fact that there is no evidence at all to support any of the charges was never even considered." *Perkins v. State of Mississippi,* p. 58.

2. *Perkins v. State of Mississippi,* p. 12.

3. *Perkins v. State of Mississippi,* p. 12.

4. "We must conclude that Douglas Huemmer and his 19 passengers were arrested and charged and now face prosecution in the State courts because—and only because—they had participated earlier in the day in the Mendenhall protests, activities immunized against official intimidation by the Civil Rights Act of 1968. Rev. Perkins, Rev. Brown and Buckley were similarly treated because—and only because—they had dared to exercise their Federally protected right to protest racial segregation in Simpson County. There is simply no other rational explanation to account for what happened." *Perkins v. State of Mississippi,* p. 51.

5. *Perkins v. State of Mississippi,* pp. 49-50.

6. *Perkins v. State of Mississippi,* pp. 11-12.

Today, John Perkins lives with his wife, Vera Mae,
in Jackson, Mississippi.
Dr. Perkins can be contacted at:

The John M. Perkins Foundation
1831 Robinson Street
Jackson, MS 39209

(601) 354-1563
www.jmpf.org

The Christian Community Development Association
can be contacted at:

3555 W. Ogden Avenue
Chicago, IL 60623

(773) 762-0994
(773) 346-0071 Fax
info@ccda.org

The Life, Legacy, and Lessons of a
CIVIL RIGHTS GIANT

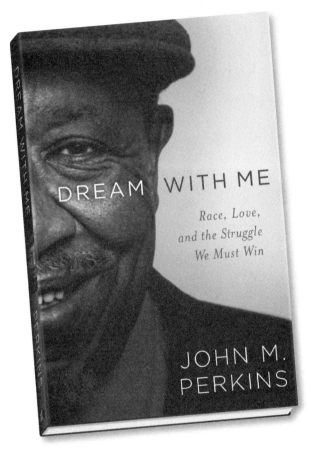

John M. Perkins has been there from the beginning. Raised by his sharecropping grandparents, Perkins fled Mississippi in 1947 after his brother was fatally shot by a police officer. He led voter registration efforts in the 1950s, worked for school desegregation in the 1960s, and was imprisoned and tortured in 1970. Through it all, he has remained determined to seek justice and reconciliation based in Christ's redemptive work.

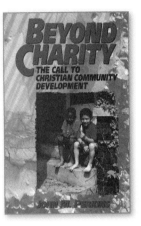
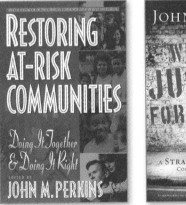
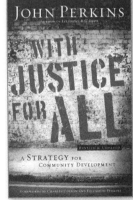